THE THIRD SHORE

大海的第三岸

ALSO EDITED BY YANG LIAN AND W.N. HERBERT

Jade Ladder (Bloodaxe Books 2010)

ALSO EDITED BY YANG LIAN

Sailor's Home (Shearsman Books 2006)

THE THIRD SHORE
大海的第三岸

CHINESE & ENGLISH-LANGUAGE POETS
IN MUTUAL TRANSLATION

中英诗人互译诗选

EDITED BY
YANG LIAN & W.N. HERBERT
主编 杨炼 威廉·赫伯特

SHEARSMAN BOOKS
&
East China Normal University Press

First published in the United Kingdom in 2013 by
Shearsman Books Ltd
50 Westons Hill Drive
Emersons Green
BRISTOL
BS16 7DF

www.shearsman.com

and in the People's Republic of China by
East China Normal University Press
3663 North Zhongshan Road
Shanghai 200062

ISBN 978-1-84861-309-6 (UK)
ISBN 978-1-84861-338-6 (PRC)

All translations are copyright
© the specified translators, 2013.

"大海的第三岸" copyright © Yang Lian, 2013.

'On the Rising Beach. Translation as Metaphor'
copyright © W.N. Herbert, 2013

The original poems in this volume, both Chinese and English, remain in the copyright of their authors and are copyright © 2013, except where listed otherwise in the Acknowledgements. Full details of the sources of the original English poems, and the permissions to reprint them, where applicable, may be found in the Acknowledgements on pages 228-229.

All rights reserved.

目录　CONTENTS

　　　　　　Yang Lian: The Third Shore　　　　　11
17　　序言1　大海的第三岸——杨炼

　　　　W.N. Herbert: On the Rising Beach. Translation as Metaphor　21
31　　序言2　高高升起的海滩：翻译之为隐喻——威廉．赫伯特

中诗英译　CHINESE INTO ENGLISH

姜涛 / Jiang Tao
40　　空军一号 / Air Force One [AS]　　41

冷霜 / Leng Shuang
42　　小夜曲 / Serenade [EG]　　43

唐晓渡 / Tang Xiaodu
44　　五月的蔷薇 / May Rose [AD]　　45
46　　镜 / Mirror [WNH]　　47
46　　叫出你的名字 / I cry out your name [WNH]　　47
48　　无题 / Untitled [WNH]　　49
50　　无题（之三）/ Part 3 of an untitled poem [FS]　　51

王小妮 / Wang Xiaoni
52　　一块布的背叛 / Betraying Cloth [PP]　　53
54　　台风四首 / Four Typhoon Poems [PP]　　55
58　　在威尔士（选二）/ *from* Wales in June [PP]　　59
60　　月光白得很 / White Moon [PP]　　61

西川 / Xi Chuan

62	巨兽 / Monster [AD]	63
64	我奶奶 / My Grandma [WNH]	65
64	奶奶 / Grandma [WNH]	65
66	佩玲 / Pei Ling [WNH]	67
68	皮肤颂 / Ode to Skin [PP]	69
70	题王希孟青绿山水长卷《千里江山图》/ After Wang Ximeng's Blue and Green Horizontal Landscape Scroll, A Thousand Miles of Rivers and Mountains' [AS]	71

萧开愚 / Xiao Kaiyu

72	留赠拉斐尔 / A Gift of Words for Raffael Keller [GS]	73
74	一次抵制 / One Resistance [GS]	75
76	山坡 / Hillside [PP]	77

严力 / Yan Li

78	中国抽屉 / The Chinese Drawers [AS]	79
80	输掉了 / Lost [WNH]	81

杨炼 / Yang Lian

82	个人地理学 / Personal Geography [AD]	83
84	鬼魂奏鸣曲 / Ghost Sonatas [PP]	85
88	饕餮之问 / Questions about the Demon Taotie [PP]	89
90	一粒葵花籽的否定句 / A Sunflower Seed's Lines of Negation [WNH]	91
92	散步者 / Stroller [WNH]	93
94	紫郁金宫：慢板的一夜 / A Night in the Purple Tulip Palace (Adagio) [WNH]	95
96	蝴蝶——纳博科夫 / Butterfly – Nabokov [JW]	97
98	蝴蝶——柏林 / Butterfly – Berlin [JW]	99

杨小滨 / Yang Xiaobin

100	目的论 / Teleology [JG]	101
102	裸露 / Nude [JG]	103
104	景色与情节 / The Setting and the Plot [JG]	105
106	离题的情歌 / Love Song Gone Awry [JG]	107
108	信件，面包，书签 / Three Short Poems [JG]	109

于坚 / Yu Jian

112	在西部荒野中看见火车 / Watching a Train in the Western Wilderness [WNH]	113

臧棣 / Zang Di

114	自我表现协会 / The Self-Expression Association [ME]	115
116	生活是怎么炼成的丛书 / How Life is Smelted [NA]	117
118	牵线人丛书 / A Puppeteer [NA]	119

翟永明 / Zhai Yongming

120	菊花灯笼漂过来 / The chrysanthemum lantern is floating over me [PP]	121
122	第六月 / Jingan Village, June [PP]	123
124	唐朝书生 / Scholars of the Tang Dynasty [SO]	125

张炜 / Zhang Wei

126	松林 / Pine Forest [PC]	127

周瓒 / Zhou Zan

128	慢 / Slowness [WNH]	129
128	未名湖 / Nameless Lake [WNH]	129
130	灰喜鹊 / Jay [PP]	131

ENGLISH INTO CHINESE　　英诗中译

Nick Admussen / 安敏轩

135	Road Trip / 驾车旅行 [臧棣 译]	134
135	Medical Thriller / 医疗惊悚 [臧棣 译]	134

Tony Barnstone / 托尼·巴恩斯通

137	Hair / 毛发 [明迪 译]	136
137	Break Up with Him (A How-to Manual) / 跟他绝交 [明迪 译]	136
139	Death / 死亡 [明迪 译]	138
139	Worn / 旧 [臧棣 译]	138

Breyten Breytenbach / 汴庭博

141	Departure / 启程 [杨炼 译]	140

Polly Clark / 波丽·克拉克

143	My Education at the Zoo / 我的动物园学历 [杨炼 译]	142
145	Cheng Du Massage / 成都按摩 [翟永明 译]	144
147	My Life, the Sea / 我的生活，海 [翟永明 译]	146
147	Beijing / 北京 [唐晓渡 译]	146
149	Swan / 天鹅 [周瓒 译]	148
151	Women / 女人 [周瓒 译]	150
153	My Life With Horses / 与马共生 [周瓒 译]	152

Jennifer Crawford / 简妮芬·克劳馥

155	A Tempo / 回旋 [杨炼 译]	154

Antony Dunn / 安东尼·邓恩

157	Flea Circus / 跳蚤马戏团 ［周瓒 译］	156
157	Lepidopterist / 蝴蝶专家 ［杨炼 译］	156
159	Unsaid / 未说的话 ［唐晓渡 译］	158

W.N. Herbert / 威廉·赫伯特

161	A Midsummer Light's Nighthouse / 仲夏灯之夜塔 ［杨炼 译］	160
163	Shields Vixen / 庇护雌狐 ［周瓒 译］	162
165	Tyne Tunnel / 泰恩河隧道 ［周瓒 译］	164
167	Forgive the Flies / 原谅苍蝇 ［唐晓渡 译］	166
167	Ghost / 鬼魂 ［唐晓渡 译］	166
169	Grandparents / 祖父母 ［唐晓渡 译］	168
169	Border Cow / 边界母牛 ［唐晓渡 译］	168
171	Slow Animals Crossing / 慢动物穿行 ［杨炼 译］	170
173	Santiniketan / 桑蒂尼科坦 ［杨炼 译］	172
175	A Difficult Horse / 一匹很难的马 ［杨炼 译］	174

Sean O'Brien / 肖恩·奥布莱恩

177	Cities / 城市 ［西川 译］	176
179	Europeans / 欧洲人 ［西川 译］	178
181	Tables and Chairs / 桌和椅 ［杨炼 译］	180
183	Another Country / 另一个国家 ［杨炼 译］	182

Pascale Petit / 帕斯卡尔·帕蒂

185	My Father's Body / 我父亲的身体 ［周瓒 译］	184
187	Self-Portrait with Fire Ants / 有火蚁的自画像 ［周瓒 译］	186
189	The Snake House / 蛇屋 ［周瓒 译］	188
189	The Strait-Jackets / 约束衣 ［周瓒 译］	188
191	Atlas Moth / 地图蛾 ［杨炼 张炜 译］	190
193	Unearthly Languages / 神奇的语言 ［杨炼 张炜 译］	192
195	The Mirror Orchid / 镜兰 ［杨炼 译］	194

Fiona Sampson / 菲奥娜·辛普森

201	Common Prayer / 共同的祈祷 [唐晓渡 译]	200

Arthur Sze / 施加彰

209	The Negative / 底片 [西川 译]	208
211	Horse Face / 马脸 [西川 译]	210
211	Pig's Heaven Inn / 猪西天客栈 [杨炼 译]	210
213	Looking Back on the Muckleshoot Reservation from Galisteo Street, Santa Fe / 从圣达菲市加利斯泰欧街回望马柯舒特印第安保留地 [西川 译]	212
215	The Moment of Creation / 混沌初开 [严力 译]	214

George Szirtes / 乔治·塞尔特斯

217	Water / 水 [杨炼 译]	216
219	Madhouse / 疯人院 [杨炼 译]	218
221	We love life whenever we can / 只要我们可以纵情地生活 [萧开愚 译]	220
221	The Best of All Possible Worlds / 所有世界里最好的那个 [萧开愚 译]	220
223	Some Sayings about the Snake / 关于蛇的一些谚语 [萧开愚 译]	222

Joshua Weiner / 约书亚·维尔纳

225	Found Letter / 寻回的信 [杨炼 译]	224
227	Cricket / 蛐蛐 [杨炼 译]	226

228	Acknowledgements	228
230	Index of Translators into English	230
230	Index of Translators into Chinese	230
231	Index of Poets	231

Introduction

The Third Shore: Poet to Poet Dialogic Translation
An Anthology of Chinese & English Poetry

Yang Lian

"Poetry is untranslatable", says the cliché. Even people who are hardly specialists in the field can quote Robert Frost's dictum, "Poetry is what gets lost in translation", which is so widely known that it has even provided the title for a Hollywood movie. But on a superficial examination, is the truth of these assertions open to challenge? To go deeper, the facts are these: a translation is not the original text, nor need it attempt to duplicate the original. The translation of a poem must itself be a poem, and must be another *different* poem. It will be an alloy, jointly forged by the original poet and the poet-translator together. The more elegant and tightly-structured the original, the greater will be the demands on the translation, and the greater the difficulty of forging that alloy. "Untranslatable"? "Lost in translation"? It's not that simple. We ought really to be asking how we translate poetry, how we might face the impossible—or even, how we might begin from what is impossible.

Walter Benjamin was a critic of surpassing insight. He called translation "The Third Language", because a translation is neither the same as the original, nor the same as the normal foreign-language of other texts, for it is something unique, something set apart from either, just as bronze forged from copper and tin overcomes the brittleness of copper and the softness of tin to become both hard and pliable, as if it has become a new element—and that allowed the great artists of the 2nd millennium BC Shang dynasty to cast their magnificent masterworks in bronze. To take a more realistic figure of speech, translation is not felling trees, but planting them: felled trees hauled to another site are dead, and will remain so, but a tree-planter is a kind of diver, who dives from leaf-tips through veins and trunk to roots back down to the source of a work of art, and from that experience of the moment of creation, brings back a total understanding of the work's structure, then grows the tree of the translation in another tongue. These two different trees sharing a single root are not, of course, identical, but they are living likenesses of each other. "The Third Language" appears to say this: the vast ocean of poetry has more than two shores, for it has a third one too. The dialogue—positive, benign, virtuous—between poet and translator, in that it allows the essential elements of both languages to be stripped bare, is the optimum formula for the reinvention of both. This is a chemical reaction that is beautiful, miraculous, tortuous and circuitous, and no-one who has not witnessed it can understand the wonder of it. Hence, the eyes of the famous presenter of a BBC literature show widened in surprise when I said that there is both loss and gain in poetry translation.

There is a proud tradition of Chinese poetry in English, and it extends to the two extremes of Arthur Waley's graceful fluency and Ezra Pound's conceptual originality. The 7th–10th century Tang poems that Waley translated are universally acknowledged to be beautiful English poems, with their carefully structured metres, rhythms, and forms, the very image of poems from the hand of a native English speaker. Perhaps the daunting nature of the formal difficulties involved gave him a tendency to avoid the challenge of "fighting on two fronts", and he was at his happiest translating the gratuitously fluent verse of Bai Juyi and other poets like him. In direct contrast, the great poet Pound's interests were precisely focussed on the abstruse nature of linguistics itself. Out of the structure of Chinese characters, he created his concept of the image, emphasising the use of specific, concrete images to embody thought, and so at one fell swoop he changed the whole face of English poetry. While Rilke was still waxing lyrical in German over non-specific images like The Angel and The Rose, T.S. Eliot had already broken through to

> When the evening is spread out against the sky
> (like a patient etherized upon a table)

Though they could not have known it, these two great masters, Waley and Pound, had opened the door to interaction between Chinese and English in today's globalised context. Chinese and English—one with an unbroken 3,000 years of creative transformation from within, and the other, the international medium of exchange, spread across almost the entire surface of the earth. (And who, on the streets of Beijing today, can leave another without uttering *Bye-bye*?) Now, the ideological significance of the interaction between Chinese and English has far surpassed the significance of either language alone: by making apparent the plight of the world we all live in, it has inspired all of us to find our own answers to the predicament we are in. This dialogue between time and space, arising from collision, conjecture and convergence, is the very being of 21st-century humanity.

The title of this preface, *The Third Shore of the Sea*, aims to point out the two levels on which poetry probes the deep sea: firstly, the poems as concrete objects; secondly, their prototypes—the life of a human rooted in a spiritual predicament. In 21st century China, tossed by storm after storm, there isn't even calm water to be had, far less any port. More than that, though, in this world of enforced global profiteering, cynicism and frivolity, what culture is still untarnished, the elegance of its days still intact? Any poem in any language is a deep-sea explorer penetrating its own vast ocean with the quivering probe of language, registering every sea-floor earthquake with its remote-sensing telemetry. If poets translate each other's work, this dialogic translation is the gentle piercing of that probe's point. "Dialogic translation" is a very general term here, allowing as it does for more than the classical one-on-one that 'poet to poet' might seem to imply, and including in its purview every possibility of encounters between Chinese and English. It is this broader sense of "one-on-one" that more exactly accords with its basic meaning. The precious trees sharing a single root spring from Life turning back to Life to let humans return to a radical understanding of each other. So this book is no mere jejune tale of cultural sightseeing, but rather the outcome of a community that was destined to come into being. So poetry, by opening this up and giving feedback to its creators, becomes worthy of the rank and title of "The Unique Mother Tongue".

The work selected for this anthology represents a brief summary of several years of poetic exchange between Chinese and English: in 2004, poets met for the first time to co-translate at the Wansongpu Academy in Shandong Province; in 2005; the dialogic translation was held at the Cove Park artists' retreat in Scotland; in 2006, the ZhongKun Poetry Foundation organised a trip into the Pamir Mountains in Central Asia, which gave the poets more chances to explore both the idea and the project; in 2007, the translation dialogue was organised by Huangshan District in Anhui Province (I still remember a delightful moment when the Nigerian poet Odia Omeifun and I compared the musicality of African oral literatures with the tones of the Chinese language); in 2008 the Yellow Mountain Poetry Festival took place in both Wales and London—this was the world's first-ever Chinese-English poetry festival, and English-speaking poets came from the UK, the USA, New Zealand and Nigeria, showing how English writing has been transformed by contact with different cultures. The most significant activity since then has been from 2008 to 2012, when I and the Scottish poet W.N. Herbert entered into an alliance with the doyen of contemporary Chinese poetry in English translation, Brian Holton, and the Chinese literary critic Qin Xiaoyu, to produce *Jade Ladder*, an anthology of contemporary Chinese poetry in English. *Jade Ladder* runs to almost 400 pages, and in its choice of original poems, its overall structure, and even in the worked fullness of its translations, it is an "Extreme Book". Through the poetry it presents, it opens up, layer by layer, China's present reality, thought and culture. The book is in six parts, each corresponding to one poetic form:

LYRIC POEMS: directly instituting a dialogue with China's most important poetic tradition;
NARRATIVE POEMS: confronting the greatest weakness of Chinese poetry;
NEO-CLASSICAL POEMS: formalist, and proud of it;

SEQUENCES: a profound statement of how structure completes thought;
EXPERIMENTAL POEMS: conceptual art in Chinese characters;
LONG POEMS: the penetration of every ocean current from the sea-floor of linguistics, upward to a panoramic view of current tempests and storms.

Jade Ladder may be thought of as a mind-map of China through the last thirty years, or, as Fiona Sampson, editor of *Poetry Review*, the UK's premier poetry journal, put it when commending the Yellow Mountain Poetry Festival in an e-mail to me, "Every detail is built on a profound understanding of poetry". This base of detailed understanding is what has allowed dialogic translation to happen over the last few years. I have called this series of steadily deepening activities the Art & Thought Project. Without it, the great and rapidly-changing book of China would be impossible to open, let alone understand. Poetry gives us a form with which to handle life. We can slip in and taste our partner's ocean via translation, to see more clearly where we stand. And, oh, how happy we are in the bodies of flying fish, as we stir up the waves of both oceans!

No need to be shy about it: when poets translate poetry there are both strengths and weaknesses. Very few poets can be dignified with the title of "translator" because, and there is no way to avoid saying this, our foreign-language skills are limited. But, and this is a point to note, our strength is in our lightning-quick grasp and profound comprehension of any poetry whatever. This resembles another proposition of mine, that poetry is "a tower built from the top downward". This profound comprehension pours down and awakens every organ in the poet's body, opening it up to language. A string of MUSTs: harsh and exacting reading, merciless interrogation, re-created sorrows and joys. An infinite number of WHYs: why is this structure needed, why is this rhythm needed? How are meaning and form interacting? The poet, used to flying along on his bicycle and choosing any route he pleases, has now become an engine driver, destined to collide with every rock on the rails! Our work is the opposite of the cute posing that most people imagine, as it actually involves a lot of dull, unthinking effort. Two poets, with sometimes an interpreter added for the express delivery of language, go head to head and eyeball to eyeball, notebooks in hand, terrified lest the slightest nuance is missed. In what sense is this "reading"? It's clearly an operating theatre, where image after image, line after line, the flesh and the bones of a dissected poem are exposed, until, with a puff of magic, we bring it back to life again! What does it feel like to detonate a poem? What is its historical background, its literary inheritance, its cultural challenge? The right of explication is now out of the creator's hands, because this invasive probing of dialogic translation is no less professional than the author's own. Anyone who tries to hide behind the excuse that "poetry is untranslatable", or who hides behind the images and plays dumb, will not escape this microscope. The two key words here are PROFOUND and PROFESSIONAL—note the euphony here—and for both the translator and the poet being translated they bring an equal test. To see your own work subject to the scrutiny of another—how can that not be significant? Does evaluation smash it into smithereens? Or does one ocean go surging into the other? The results of these tests are really interesting too: the fewer the ideas in the original, the easier will translation be. Any translator can arbitrarily cook something up from a heap of raw material, and it is often the case that the translation has more flavour than the original, but on the other hand, an original whose form and connotation are crafted with precision will have the translator racking his or her brains, caught between conflicting priorities, and more often than not feeling he or she is not up to the task at all. To take an example of my own, the very intelligent Pascale Petit grabbed my attention when she said, "Only you could translate *Mirror Orchid*", but it wasn't until I got my hands on it that I saw what she meant: the long lines reminiscent of Saint-John Perse, the gorgeous and complex images with their intriguing mixture of tension and release, and all controlled by the dexterity and rigour of English grammar—these unerringly show up the Achilles heel of the free and unfixed grammar of Chinese. Take this line, for example—

the fossil-flowers with stone petals and sulphur stems

here, the F and S sounds are entwined in euphony, like two rattlesnakes. In response to this, all I could do in Chinese was

huashi hua you shihua ban

Sean O'Brien's acerbic political poem 'Another Country' is given an exquisite beauty and delicacy by the use of strict rhyme, and I wasn't going to be beaten at that game. In George Szirtes' 'Water', the AB rhyme scheme and the many caesuras are so meticulously and systematically intertwined that the translated text must mark and shadow every one of these moves from beginning to end. His 'Madhouse' is another beauty: in it, a poet of Jewish extraction unexpectedly uses the German word *Gesundheit* to comic effect. Good lord, what was I to do with that? Then the penny dropped, and I used the kind of broken Chinese the Imperial Japanese Army used in WWII.

The majority of poets involved in dialogic translation are in their thirties, forties and mid-fifties, so, because of their age, they are self-aware users of language, well supplied with experience of life, mature in their thought and creative powers. More important, though, is the globalised context (or predicament?) of our own personal experience; the profound level of exchange this makes possible is not just important, but indispensable. For as long as humans have made poetry, poets have been aware of one thing: *there is only one sea*, and you either dive in and swim deeper into it, or you simply don't get wet. Dialogic translation implies mutual assessment: with reference to so many multi-faceted cultural systems, can a poet's creative work still be "valid"? The steamroller of globalisation is flattening all the previous supports for communities: ethnicities, nations, cultures, languages, ideologies—even the dividing line between East and West—until all that is left is

> A man taking the road shoulder to shoulder with the universe[1]

Yet this road is not solely one that leads toward the outside world, because it is even more an inward one, for, in the final analysis, all the burden of the world falls on the shoulders of the individual. And this is the true significance of dialogic translation: as we weigh each and every word, sharing layer after layer of meaning, then here, in the deep places of every culture our own personal powers are interrogated. This focus on the Third Language makes manifest the Third Shore of the sea, transcending the limits of geography, as well as the narrow limits of culture-bound psychologies, and exemplifying the common course of our shared humanity. Now, is The Third Shore of the sea excavated from the sea-floor, and simultaneously surveying us from the heavens? I have described the ecology of the internet as like the ocean, with culture the boat, and poetry the ballast in its hold. Poetry keeps the boat stable, preventing it from rolling and yawing or drifting with the current. On the ocean's Third Shore all you need is to think a poem is good for it to become your own. Any volunteer, through writing, translation, criticism, reading, even a beginner whose first lessons have touched on translation, can land here, right on The Third Shore of the Sea.

IT/IS/IN/SIDE/US

An unbroken and forever unfolding shoreline that transcends time and space is even now weaving a worldwide web of co-translating poets. Here is the genuine, the magnificent Art & Thought Project. Faced with that, this anthology of dialogic translation into Chinese and English is only a first attempt, only a beginning.

Translated by Brian Holton

---

[1] From my own unpublished 'Narrative Poem'

大海的第三岸

——中英诗人互译诗选序

杨炼

"诗不可译",这是一句套话。稍专业点儿的人,会引用美国诗人佛洛斯特的名言:"诗就是翻译中失去的"。此话如此流行,以至好莱坞都借它做了电影名。但,它们真像表面看来那么不容置疑吗?深究一下,事实是:译文并非原作,也无须企图复制原作。诗之译文,必须是诗,又必须是"另一首诗"。它是一种合金,由原作诗人和译作诗人共同浇铸而成。原作越精美严谨,对译作要求越高,铸造"合金"的难度越大。"不可译"、"翻译即失去",其实太简单了。该问的是:怎么译?如何迎向那"不可能"——且从不可能开始?瓦尔特·本雅明总是聪颖过人。他称翻译为"第三种语言",既不同于原文,又不同于普通外文,而是两者之外独具一格的东西。正像铜锡混合成青铜,避开了铜之脆和锡之软,却变得既硬且韧,像另一种元素,让伟大的商代艺术家,熔铸成华美的镇国之宝。换个实在些的比喻,翻译不是砍树,而是植树。砍下的树桩,挪到另一片土地上,也死定了。而植树者是一种"潜泳者",她(他)沿着叶梢、叶脉、树干、树根潜回作品源头,又从原创经验中,带着对原作构成的全部理解,用另一种语言生长出译文之树。这同根异株,形象当然不同,却又活生生一派神似。"第三种语言",好像在说:诗歌的大海不仅有两岸,更有第三岸。它在诗人和译者良性对话中,让不同语言敞开自身,按最佳配方被再"发明"一次。这化学之变美丽、神奇、迂回曲折,非亲历者不能尽享其妙。由是,一次英国BBC文学采访中,当我说:"诗歌翻译同时是失去和获得",竟令那位著名主持人惊奇地瞪大了漂亮的眼睛。

中英诗歌翻译的"传统"堪称丰富,且代表了译诗的两种极端方式:阿瑟·威利式的文笔流畅和庞德式的观念独创。前者翻译的唐诗,有公认的英诗之美,其韵律、节奏、形式工整,活似出自英语母语诗人之手。大约因为形式挑战的严峻,威利稍稍回避在思想、文笔上"双线作战",而更乐意翻译白居易之类平白流畅的作品。和他相反,大诗人庞德的兴趣,恰恰聚焦于最艰深的语言学本质。他从汉字的构成引申出"意象"观念,强调用具体、结实的形象涵括思想,一举改造了英诗整个面目。当德语的里尔克还津津于"天使"、"玫瑰"等空泛象征,英语的艾略特已砸下"黄昏像个麻醉了的病人躺在手术台上"了。 威利和庞德两位大师并不知道,他们几乎超前一个世纪,开启了今天全球化语境里的中英交流之门。中文和英文,一个三千年从未间断自身之内的创造性转型,一个作为国际通用交流媒介,覆盖了地球上最大的面积(唉,如今中国街头,不冒一声"败败",谁还会分手告别呢?)。因此,中英交流的思想意义,远超出两个语种，而令全球化处境显形，更启发着每个人应对这处境的方式。这场时间和空间的对话，碰撞、探测、交汇出的，正是二十一世纪人的存在。

这篇序言《大海的第三岸》，意在指出，诗歌探测大海的两个层次：深入诗作和它们的"原版"——在精神困境中思索的人生。中国的二十世纪，除了风暴还是风暴，别说港湾，连平静些的海面也没有。但不止于此，今天，被全球利益化、玩世不恭化逼近（注意：这"逼近"，是被逼着互相靠近之意）的世界上，哪个文化能洁身自好、优雅独处？用任何语言写下的每首诗，都是一架深海探测器，用语言这根震颤的探针，穿透自身的大海，遥感遥测着每个大海的海底地震。诗人互译，就是探针尖端的轻轻一碰。这里的"互译"是广义的，它不拘泥于固定诗人的"一对一"，而更着眼于中英两个语种之间，"相遇"的各种可能性。一种更广义、却恰和其本意的"一对一"。"同根异株"的诗歌玉树，来自人生又还原为人生，让人类在"根"上互相读懂。因此，这本书绝非泛泛的文化观光，而其实是一个命运共同体。诗歌以其开阔，回馈创造者，并荣膺"唯一的母语"之名。

精选在这本诗选中的作品，堪称一种小结，展示了过去历年来中英诗人交流的成果。简单罗列的大项目计有：二零零四年，中英诗人首次在中国山东万松浦书院互译。二零零五年，在苏格兰"湾园"艺术中心互译。二零零六年，中坤诗歌基金会组织的帕米尔之旅上，诗人对此项目的深入探讨。二零零七年，在安徽黄山地区组织的中英诗人互译对话（我还记得，和尼日利亚诗人奥斐曼比较非洲口头文学音乐性和汉语音调的那个美妙瞬间！）。二零零八年，在英国威尔士和伦敦举行的"黄山诗歌节"——世界上首次在中英两语种间举行的诗歌节上，英语诗人来自英、美、新西兰、尼日利亚，展示出被不同文化背景"改造"了的英文书写。之后的大动作，是二零零八年到二零一二年，历时四年多，由我和英国诗人威廉·赫伯特（William Herbert）牵头，由当今中诗英译最强译者霍布恩（Brian Holton）和中文诗歌批评家秦晓宇加盟，共同主编的《玉梯》英译当代中文诗选。它厚达近四百页，从原作选择、全书结构，到译文完成度，都堪称一部"极端之书"。它通过诗歌，翻开了当代中国现实、思想、文化的一切层次。全书六个部分，基于六种诗歌形式：抒情诗（直接和古典中国最重要的诗歌传统建立"创造性对话"）；叙事诗（直面传统汉语诗的最弱项）；组诗（以结构完成思想的深层表述）；新古典诗（骄傲的"形式主义"）；实验诗（汉字观念艺术）；长诗（从语言学的海底、穿透层层海流，直到现实的风暴尽收眼底）。《玉梯》被称为过去三十年中国的"思想地图"，恰如英国资深诗刊《诗歌评论》的主编菲奥娜·辛普森对"黄山诗歌节"的称赞："每个细节都建立在对诗歌的深刻理解上。"没错。因为这"理解"的地基，正是几年来进行的诗人互译。这一系列持续深化的活动，被我称为"思想——艺术项目"。没有它，急剧变化的"中国"这部大书，很难被打开，更别说读懂了。诗歌其实在赋予我们把握人生的形式。通过翻译，让我们潜入、品尝着对方那个大海的滋味，更清晰了自己之所在。呵，同时拨动两个大海的波浪，我们飞鱼似的身体多么畅快！

毋庸讳言，诗人译诗有弱项有长项。弱项是外语能力。很少有诗人顶着"翻译家"的头衔，因此，无需避讳我们外语的局限。但，更该关注的，是我们的长项：那就是对任何诗意疾如闪电的深彻领悟。这颇像我的另一个命题："一座向下修建的塔"。那领悟，自顶上灌下，驱策着诗人的浑身器官，向语言敞开。一串"不得不"：苛刻的阅读，残酷的追问，再创造的痛苦和快感。无数"为什么"：为什么一定是这个结构、这个节奏？形式和意味如何互动？在随意找路的自行车上飞翔惯了的诗人，现在成了火车司机，铁轨上的任何石头，只能撞上去！我们的工作，与别人想象的漂亮身段相反，下的其实是极笨的功夫。两个诗人（有时加一个快递语言的"通译"）头挨头，眼盯眼，紧抓笔记本，生怕漏掉任何一丝信息。这哪是阅读？明明是手术室，一个个意象、一行行句子，解剖一首诗的肌理骨骼，还要再吹一口仙气，让它活过来！触发这首诗的人生感受是什么？它的历史背景、文学传承、文化挑战是什么？阐释权并不总在原作诗人手里，因为"探针"刺探得同样专业。谁想靠一句"诗不能解释"推托，或靠躲进意象游戏藏拙，逃不过那架显微镜。这里的两个关键词：一，深刻的（Profound）；二，专业的（Professional）——请注意它们的英语谐音——令无论翻译或被译的诗人，同样经受考验。好在，我们做这件事的前提，就是乐意经受这考验。看看自己的作品，在他者审视下，还是否有意义？是被审读砸成了碎片？抑或一个大海汹涌进另一个大海？检验结果也确实有趣：原作越缺乏想法，翻译越容易。一堆原料，可供译者任意"炒菜"，且经常译作比原作更有味道。反之，从形式到内涵精密讲究的原作，则逼得译者绞尽脑汁、左冲右突，还常常自叹弗如。举我自己的例子，帕斯卡尔．帕蒂很聪明，她激我："《镜兰》这首诗，只有你能翻译"。呵，拿到手才知道那句话什么意思！诗中圣．琼．佩斯式的长句，绚丽繁复又张弛有致的意象，被英语语法灵活而不失严谨地掌控着，却正点到中文语法松散的"死穴"。比如一句："the fossil-flowers with stone petals and sulphur stems"，谐音中两个"f"和六个"s"，绞缠如两条响尾蛇。我只能以中文"化石花有石花瓣"（"化石"、"石花"音响对照）来应对。尚．奥布莱恩的《另一个国家》，把一首酸涩的政治诗，用严格的韵脚变得极其精美，我也不能落了下风。乔治．塞尔特斯的《水》，韵式AB纠缠、顿数一丝不苟，译文必须全场紧逼盯人。他的《疯人院》更绝，一个犹太背景的诗人写的英语诗中，竟用上了一个令人笑不出来的德文词"身体好"，天！这怎么办？我灵光一现，把它译成了二战特色的日本侵华语——"强壮大大的"！

参与中英互译的诗人，大半是中壮年一代作者。这里有年龄因素，他们代表了一个语种的"此在"，其人生经验、思考成熟、创作能量最足。但更重要的，是我们亲历的全球化语境（我该说"困境"？），让我们懂得这深度交流，不仅重要，而且必须。自人类有诗歌史以来，诗人首次如此自觉：大海只有一个。你或者跃入它游得更深更

19

好,或者干脆就没沾水。互译的潜台词是互相检验:多重文化系统参照下,一个诗人的创作还是否"有效"?全球化的推土机,碾平了此前一切群体依托:民族、国家、文化、语种、意识形态、甚至东西方分野,只剩下"一个人和宇宙并肩上路"(拙作《叙事诗》)。而这条路,并非仅仅"向外"走向世界,更是"向内",世界的分量归根结底又都落到一个人身上。这才是互译之真义:我们字斟句酌、一层层分享的,正是每个文化深处追问自我的能量。它聚焦于这"第三种语言"中,让发现"大海的第三岸",既超越地理也超越狭隘的文化心理,而归纳出"人"共同的精神历程。那么,"第三岸"是不是正从海底和天空,同时挖掘和俯瞰着我们?我形容过,网络生态犹如大海,文化是船,而诗是船底的压舱石。诗歌稳住那条船,不准它东摇西晃、随波逐流。"大海的第三岸"上,只要你感到一首诗的"好",它就是你的。任何志愿者,写,译,评,读,哪怕初学外语擦过译诗,都正在"第三岸"上登陆。它,在,我,们,内,部。一条跨越时空、连绵不断的海岸线,正在织成诗人互译的世界网络,这才是真正的、辉煌的"思想——艺术项目"。相对它,这部中英诗人互译诗选,只是一种尝试,一个开端。

On the Rising Beach:
Translation as a Metaphor

W.N. Herbert

1

The Argentinian novelist, Andrés Neuman, had occasion to remark at a literary festival I recently attended in Cardiff, "Reading poetry is itself a kind of translation." This idea, that poetry is a medium which brings us all into the realm of the translator, is both challenging and suggestive. It implies that an act of decipherment lies at the heart of the pleasure of poetry, and also that a degree of ability to interpret may be as universal as the poetic act itself.

This anthology began eight years ago with a similar principle—that poets were sufficiently intrigued by the expressive modes and strategies of other poets to find a way of leaping the language barrier in search of greater understanding of each other's practice. The hope was that direct dialogue could lead to meaningful acts of translation, a deeper understanding of both our skills and their cultural relativism, and, ideally, publishable works in the target language.

Practically speaking, this impulse manifested itself in a trip by some UK poets to meet with Chinese writers and work on translations of each other's work in Beijing and the Wansongpu Writers' Centre in Shandong Province, then a return trip by the Chinese writers to Cove Park in the west of Scotland. The originating figures were, on the Chinese side, Yang Lian and Tang Xiaodu, together with Xi Chuan, Zhai Yongming, Zhang Wei and Zhou Zan. On the British side, Polly Clark and Julian Forrester organized, and Polly, myself, Antony Dunn and Pascale Petit took part.

On those two trips, translation went on in parallel, with the writers working both from Chinese into English, and from English into Chinese. It was a dialogue in several senses of the word, in that not only were we learning about each other's poetry and its cultural and formal background through the act of translation, but that act was itself dialogic, "Poet to Poet", as Polly called it.

This was only the first of a series of exchanges, called, variously, the Pamirs, Yellow Mountain and Yangzhou festivals. These included readings and discussions as well as translations, and involved many other writers both British, Chinese, American, Nigerian, and from New Zealand. But at the heart of each of these exchanges was a pair of writers sitting down together and learning about each other's writing and the principles behind it through the act of translation.

Several names recurred, while others joined us, including, on the English-speaking side, Murray Edmond, Forrest Gander, Robert Minhinnick, Sean O'Brien, Odia Ofeimun, Fiona Sampson, Arthur Sze, George Szirtes, Eliot Weinberger and C.D. Wright. Other Chinese writers taking part included Duo Duo, Hu Xudong, Mang Ke, Ouyang Jianghe, Wang Xaoni, Xiao Kaiyou, Yan Li, Yang Xiaobin, Yu Jian, Zang Di and Zhang Er. Not everyone translated, and not all the translations were successful, but the strong impulse to engage in dialogue about poetry drove us all.

These are distinguished names, and both the dialogues and the translation processes were so stimulating, it was inevitable that, eventually, we would think of publishing some of the results. Yang Lian and I had already collaborated on *Jade Ladder* (Bloodaxe Books, 2012), a comprehensive selection of translations into English of key poems from the last thirty years of Chinese poetry, the idea for which had arisen as a direct result of these festivals and exchanges.

But we were always aware, firstly, that the translation process had gone in both directions, and, secondly, that a large anthology like *Jade Ladder* could not focus exclusively on that process. So we decided that a second, independent book was necessary: one that included English to Chinese translations alongside Chinese to English, and one that gathered its work primarily from the Poet to Poet translation method.

That method had of course evolved over the years, not least because its application had spread. Yang Lian and other Chinese writers worked with Japanese and other poetries. Polly and Julian developed a similar project with Arab and Israeli writers; and I found myself translating from a number of other languages including Bulgarian, Farsi, Lithuanian, Somali and Turkish.

Poet to Poet changed my practice as a writer and, as an academic, became my main research area. I began travelling to translate, engaging with other organisations like Aberystwyth's Literatures Across Frontiers, Edinburgh's Scottish Poetry Library, and the London-based Poetry Translation Centre; and with other co-translators like Linda France, Richard Gwyn, Martin Orwin and Zöe Skoulding.

But both Yang Lian and myself never forgot that there was something unique about the translation process working between Chinese and English, something that informed all the other translation work we subsequently did.

The gap between the two languages and between the two cultures could not have seemed wider—English, obviously, is represented by an alphabetic system which encodes its linguistic and cultural history within its orthography, so that to read it is to reach back through etymology into layers of time.

Chinese, equally evidently, deploys thousands of characters which represent concepts and their interactions spatially through combinations of pictograms and radicals. The same characters can be used by quite distinct languages and pronounced entirely differently, while retaining much the same meaning. This, together with the fact that characters were fixed at such an historically distant time—despite efforts made by the Communist Party to reform and simplify many key characters—means that they can seem almost timeless.

The gap between the two cultures is almost as marked: Western European thinking as exemplified by English and US culture continues to empiricise wherever it can no longer colonise, to be extroverted and individualist. This it does to almost the same extent that Chinese thought has traditionally focused on the phenomenal, while creating an enclosed and hierarchically ordered social system in which China is already a world, complete unto itself. Communism almost destroyed the infrastructure of that world-view while, fundamentally, it inherited the mind-set, translating it into a unique political and industrial complex, where the Party and capitalism are, oxymoronically, one and the same thing.

Chinese literature is at once far more ancient and extensive than literature in English, and far more isolated on the far side of postmodernity, unable to establish easily connections with writers from millennia back, poets everyone has memorized but whose lives seem unimaginably alien. Thanks to those unchanging characters, everyone can read the poetry of the Tang or Song dynasties, but no-one can be entirely certain how it was pronounced.

English literature, on the other hand, manifests its distinct periods through linguistic as well as cultural or formal evolution, regularly requiring itself to be translated into its latest manifestation. Somehow, that familiarity with mutability, with relative equivalences, and with the gaps in meaning that such familiarity both opens up and conceals, gave it a flexibility that seemed fit for the task.

Somehow, when we sat down together to translate—line by line, character by character—the series of gulfs I've just described, each as sheer as the other, caused something rich and paradoxical to happen. For one thing, to discuss the surface of the language was, necessarily, to discuss its depths. For another, English's focus on its music, its long engagement with different modes of metricality, connected with Chinese's love of pattern, and its patterning of centuries of allusion.

The historicising music of English met the conceptualism of the Chinese character, and English's concept of the poetic encountered Chinese's very distinct tonal music. Each culture was mature enough in a different enough way to match the other technically as well as to contrast teleologically. There was vigorous debate because there could be real exchange: something, we realized with increasing excitement, was at stake.

2

So what was the *Poet to Poet* method, and how has it evolved over the eight or so years encompassed by this anthology? How specifically did its processes lead to a change in emphasis in how we translated poetry in both directions?

Arguably, the method has its roots in a remark by Pound from *How To Read*, where he states in typically absolute fashion:

> Another point miscomprehended by people who are clumsy at languages is that one does not need to learn a whole language in order to understand some one or some dozen poems. It is often enough to understand thoroughly the poem, and every one of the few dozen or few hundred words that compose it.

Poet to Poet translation, then, is one whereby a poet sets out to inform another poet of the full cultural significance of those "few dozen or few hundred words" from the dubious position of authority of having written them. Literary translation utilising this dialogic method was initially conducted without any preparatory literal or interlinear text, where there was a common language (almost always English).

Later it was also done between poet and poet with an accompanying interpreter, often a skilled translator or poet/translator in their own right. Sometimes, where the original poet could not be present, it was done between poet and translator. In this latter case, which clearly strains the original term, the translator tended—indeed needed—to be not only an expert in the field of literary translation, but also a close contact of the originating author, able to verify their responses through consultation.

In both the latter cases, literals tended to be used, giving rise to complications of their own, which I'll return to later.

However, in all three cases the aim remains to create a publishable text through the dynamic dialogue between writers in source and target language. This changes normal translation procedures in several significant ways.

Firstly, and most importantly, the work is usually selected by the original author. This reverses the procedure, whereby the expert translator selects from the passive canon of a foreign poetry, and thereby it also inverts the hierarchy whereby the selection of the poem can be made according to assumed ease of translation, or for ideological or aesthetic "fit" with the target culture. Chinese has for a long time been subject to a series of orientalising gestures which this method counters even though we understand it cannot entirely escape them.

This procedure has its hazards—a work may be discovered to be effectively untranslatable, or at any rate less effective in the target language. It often proves to be far harder to translate than either party realized at the outset. But these dangers are outweighed by the benefit of discovering how the originating poet wants to be represented (assuming this was a factor in their selection process—it is still of course possible for the poet to select 'easier' pieces.)

Secondly, the active presence or accessibility of the originating poet allows for a more detailed, more informed and, arguably, more accurate picture of the poem to be constructed. It at least brings out into the open the amount of second guessing any translation process must be filled with, making explicit the degree to which the translator has to consider intention as much as meaning, gesture as much as tone—because the translator can simply ask the author. This is one of those areas that feels very different depending on whether you are the translator or the translated. It is as marvellous to be able just to ask, as it is challenging to have to answer.

Thirdly, the presence of a poet fluent in the target language can mean a high level of discussion about formal issues, with the result thereby achieving more of an agreed equivalence in metrical, imagistic and, where suitable, idiomatic finish. Effectively, the Poet to Poet method allows for a strong engagement with the issue of cultural translation on the level of craft.

These three positive elements allow for an almost unique moment of shared reflection for both originating poet and poet-translator. Many of the questions one is asked as part of this process are not those one asks oneself during composition. Indeed, some such questions may need to be avoided, deliberately or instinctively, in order for composition to take place.

Equally, for the translator, this process may oblige them to reflect upon aspects of their own creative habits and perspectives in a more exteriorized and critical light, to assess whether they are indeed fit for purpose. Both writers are, after all, often encountering the different cultural weight they attach to the same literary technique, mode, or sphere of reference.

This moment in which both parties achieve however partially a conscious perspective on their own poetic procedures and creativity may be seen as a kind of secondary effect of the translation process, but it is one with huge implications for the success of the project. Depending on each party's ability briefly to escape their own milieu the dialogue mode of Poet to Poet allows, indeed causes, change to take place in their approach or practice, and the successful translation is often more dependent on the nature of this change than either party may have allowed.

To be able to let go of the poem or the practice is, effectively, not to impede transmission. This condition is the "third shore" to which we refer in our title, a place that cannot be completely governed by the poetic customs or cultural tides of either the original or the target languages.

The Scottish poet Hugh MacDiarmid, who often had to negotiate those treacherous crossings between the languages of the British Isles, referred to a similar sanctuary at once of transition and translation when in his long poem, 'In Memoriam James Joyce', he welcomes Joyce "to our *aonach*", conflating two Gaelic words—one for a meeting place or fair, and another meaning a ridge or high place.

The third shore as a point of colloquy between poets and between poetries finds its corollary in his poem 'On a Raised Beach', where the shoreline has been literally lifted above the sealine by eons of geological change, and the stones stranded on this beach symbolise an "inoppugnable reality" the poet attempts to approach through language, deploying an extraordinary extended range of scientific vocabulary and Shetlandic Norse in an attempt to translate the stones into words:

> This cat's cradle of life; this reality volatile yet undetermined;
> This intense vibration in the stones
> That makes them seem immobile to us…

This kind of intense encounter with what lies within the line, the metre, the image, the tone, the character or the word—with that which may well prove untranslatable—is the goal of the *Poet to Poet* method.

The very intensity of this dialogue, however, may sometimes contain within it the seeds of its own undoing. There is a temptation for the translated poet, reconsidering his or her own work, to use the translation to develop an idea explored through discussion, i.e. for the translation to become a means of revision. There is a similar temptation on the part of the translating poet to make sense of the poem according to their own instincts and principles, rather than having the patience to allow the meaning and style of the source text to emerge through discussion and redrafting.

This confusion of the fluidity of the draft translation with that of the compositional draft can lead to a kind of *folie à deux*, in which both poets do what they do best, composing, while believing they are acting in the best interests of the poem. This is why the dialogue is often better chaired by a translator who, like a marriage counsellor, can pull both parties back to the text at key moments. It is also why having more than one translating poet means they too can enter into dialogue about stylistic and interpretive issues in the target language, the results of which might be less individual, but they can also be more resistant to personal habit.

The ideal model for the *Poet to Poet* translation method as it has evolved might therefore be the quadrilogue, consisting of, firstly, the originating poet either present or accessible; secondly, the interpreting or intermediating poet/translator; and, thirdly and fourthly, two poets from the target language. Of course these four roles can be played by just two or three parties, but four allows for the greatest degree of engagement and objectivity.

What this evolutionary process has also given rise to is a more sophisticated understanding of the different roles played by different kinds of preparatory text. Originally, as stated above, there were none: two poets sat down together with a poem selected by the source language poet, and off they set. Gradually, the role of some form of literal translation in order to determine which poems to translate began to seem useful. But this brought its own dangers.

Literals are, naturally, never only that—a literal version of the poem, which enables work to begin. They tend to be, already, versions, often produced by writer-translators with strong aesthetic principles of their own, articulated or not, which mean they have made a series of decisions about how to produce the literal, which they then have to, but may not be in a position to, explain to the target language poet or poets. Therefore, a certain amount of this translation method—especially if the original author is not present or is not fluent in the target language—is spent assessing the literal rather than engaging with the original.

Authors of literals often feel they have already done the hard work because they have the source language expertise or know the original author well, and may have less grasp of the significance of the stage the target language poets are embarking on. It can be difficult to explain that, as is sometimes the case, their version may not be publishable in the target culture, and that an emphasis on dictionary definition or on loyalty to the author can reach a point where it becomes obstructive.

For this reason, poets working in this method often use the literal mainly to help selection, whereupon they embark on the creation of an interlinear—a word-for-word crib, preserving word order, listing synonyms, and noting cultural or stylistic issues as they arise. This construction of the interlinear is achieved specifically by a deconstruction of the literal, and directly engenders the dialogue discussed above.

3

I wrote in the introduction to *Jade Ladder* about my conviction, gained through working on that book, that translation is a fundamental aspect of any process of dialogue, not just those evidently about a transfer of meanings across languages. The transition from one era to another, from one class to another, from one gender to another, from a memory to the world-view of the present self, each involves us in a type of translation.

This is self-evidently a metaphoric use of the term "translation", but we must always be alive to the metaphors through which we conceptualise such exchanges. Many of our metaphors for translation tend to contain hierarchical assumptions, from the gendered "mother tongue" to the idea that meaning can be "lost" as though it were baggage—or rather merchandise—

in transit. And yet there is a more fundamental sense in which translation is itself metaphoric, which has a direct bearing on the processes employed and the choices made by the poets gathered in this anthology.

Translators are often supposed to work in what might be described as a metonymic manner; that is, when seeking equivalences of language, form, image or cultural reference, it is often anticipated that they will seek contiguous ones—synonyms rather than antonyms, syllabics for numbers of characters, images drawn from the same field of reference, and cultural equivalences that appear to be as "close" as possible.

But it is as often the case that what is being sought are metaphoric equivalences—words, metrics, images, references, which are "like" the original, but don't necessarily directly correspond. The likeness, as in metaphor, is made implicit by the act of creating a poem in the target language, rather than, say, writing an essay about the original poem. In a sense, the translation is itself a metaphor for the original. In I.A. Richards' terms, the original is the tenor, and the translation is the vehicle.

This relationship is, I think, particularly clear when we look at translations between English and Chinese. The dynamic between pictogram and meaning in Chinese is often metonymic, for instance the character meaning fresh, 鲜 (*xiān* in pinyin), consists of an association made from contiguous elements—the characters for two fresh things, "fish" and "sheep" (鱼, *yú* and 羊, *yáng*).

By contrast, for the English speaker, "fresh" delivers its associations by dint of being an Old English monosyllable. That is, whether we are aware of its etymology or not, most English speakers register the directness of the sound and link it to its meaning in a way we might not so readily do with "neoteric" or "uncontaminated". Synonyms in English come from different sources that we don't always recognize as contiguous, and in fact can experience as contrasting.

When we think about the relation between 鲜 and "fresh" therefore, we are thinking metaphorically about how a spatial relationship between characters can resemble a meaning built up through complementary or contrasting linguistic roots, i.e. a temporal relationship. This is, I believe, what the poet Yu Jian meant when he said at a recent festival in Nanjing, "The Chinese character cannot be translated." He didn't mean that a kind of translation did not take place, but rather that translating Chinese makes us think laterally about equivalence itself.

To think of translation as a search for metaphors as much as a search for meanings is to note that *likeness* may be something subtly different from *similarity*. Twins can resemble each other exactly but have different natures, while two strangers can contrast in every way while recognizing—or at least agreeing—that they are in some way fundamentally alike.

Translation in this sense is a kind of leap of faith which we can only commit to if trust has been established between translated and translating poets: they must have faith in each other's judgement as poets beyond the limits of their grasp of each other's language and culture. *Poet to Poet* translation, then, is a relationship rather than an infallible method, one in which we hope to recognize and value likeness.

This recognition of likeness occurred again and again in the creation of this book, as poets in both languages acknowledged that each other's engagement with their culture's politics, history and prosody was not just similar to their own, or not just simplistically operating in parallel, but felt as though it were the same engagement. The evidence was as simple as finding you were as fascinated by your fellow poet's problematic or otherwise relationship with his or her canon as you were by your own, and indeed as he or she was by your own.

It was certainly the case that many of the poets from Britain responded strongly to the way in which Chinese writers were renegotiating their relationship with avant-garde techniques (often imported from US poetics) through a radical exploration of their classical heritage, in which, on the one hand, no simplistic direct link to that heritage was assumed to exist, nor, on the other, in the wake of the horrors of the Cultural Revolution, was an absolute break with that past considered either desirable or possible.

This was, some of us felt, not unlike the continued negotiation that had gone on throughout twentieth and twenty-first century poetry written in Britain and Ireland between what was interpreted as experimental and traditional poetries and poetics. Having as broad a variety of formal resources as theoretical approaches seemed to both sets of poets to be of something like the same importance.

This sense of shared values and of common commitment to a method of translation that places such emphasis on dialogue may, it is hoped, help to mitigate a final imposition that anthologies of this kind make upon their contents and contributors.

Our cultures do not have a detailed awareness of each other as contemporary entities, especially when it comes to the field of poetry. The temptation, therefore, especially for readers of English contemplating the vastness of Chinese culture, but also for Chinese readers considering the wide variety of Englishes from US to UK to Indian, Australian, and so on, is always to employ a sort of thinking by synecdoche, that rhetorical device whereby the part is held to stand for the whole. "I shall never read everything," we think, refusing to admit the thought even as it arises, "therefore, this poem shall represent this poet; this poet shall stand for that cultural movement; and this anthology shall be adequate for the entire medium of poetry in that language."

This anthology seeks to displace that act of substitution by moving in two directions at the one time. Each language presents to the reader a portrait of itself and a picture of the other as selected by that other. These two images simultaneously encourage comparison and contrast. They are in dialogue with each other exactly as the poets who translated each other were in dialogue. They in fact represent that process as much as they represent their respective cultures, and they suggest limitations: this type of anthology can only consist of that part of each culture which is prepared or practically able to enter into this kind of dialogue: there will be many who are not, or cannot do so.

This is the sort of limitation many writers will recognize as a great liberation: the technical restriction that obliges invention, and thereby enables you to escape from other, more doctrinaire constraints. We do not, I think, want to represent our cultures in quite so straightforward a manner as a synecdochic reading implies. Rather we wish to explore what we can do as writers and translators freed from this sort of representation into a zone where communication, with each other, with our own, and with each other's audience, is the key element. In that zone, if the quality of the original writing and of the translation is high enough, both writers and audiences will create their own understanding of our respective poetries, their links and contrasts, their evident particularity and their possible universality. They will, in effect, land upon the third shore.

高高升起的海滩：翻译之为隐喻

威廉·赫伯特

1.

阿根廷小说家安德烈·纽曼在他最近于卡地夫参加的一个文学节上曾说，"阅读诗歌，自身就是一种翻译。"这一关于诗作为媒介，将我们大家带入译者的领域的观念，既充满挑战，又富于暗示。它意味着，一种解码的行为，处于诗之愉悦的核心；而诠释的能力，就像诗歌本身那样触目皆是。

这本诗集发端于八年前，始于同样的准则——诗人们尝试逾越语言障碍，满足自己对其他诗人创作的强烈好奇心和理解渴望：通过直接对话，导向富有意义的翻译行为，一种对我们的技巧和他们的文化更深的理解；达到更理想状态时，能以译文出版作品。

现实的层面上，两次旅行彰显了这冲动。英国作家造访了北京和位于山东省的万松浦书院，与中国作家一同翻译了各自的作品。中国作家随即回访苏格兰"湾园艺术中心"。最初几位作家是中国方面的杨炼、唐晓渡、西川、翟永明、张炜和周瓒。英国方面则由波丽·克拉克、朱利安·弗里斯特担任组织工作，波丽、我自己、安东尼·邓恩和帕斯卡尔·葩蒂参与。

两次行程中，翻译工作平行展开，诗人们进行中英文互译。这是一场几个层面意义上的对话。因为我们不但通过翻译学习对方的诗歌及其文化和形式背景，翻译行为本身也是对话的，正如波丽所称，"诗人对诗人"的。

这是也被称作"帕米尔"和"黄山诗歌节"系列交流活动的首站。系列交流活动包括朗诵、讨论以及翻译，参与其中的其他多位作家分别来自英国，中国，美国，尼日利亚，新西兰。每项交流活动的核心，是一对作家一同坐下来，在互译中一道学习对方的写作及其创作背后的原则。

有几个名字反复出现，新的名字不断加入进来。其中包括：英语诗人方面的默里·埃德蒙、弗里斯特·甘德、罗伯特·米希尼克、欧迪亚·奥菲蒙、菲欧娜·桑普森、施家彰、乔治·塞尔斯特、艾略特·魏恩伯格和C·D·赖特。中文诗人还有：陈东东、胡旭东、芒克、欧阳江河、王小妮、萧开愚、严力、臧棣和张洱。诗歌对话的冲动，趋迫着我们每一个人。

这都是些令人尊敬的名字。翻译对话过程如此令人感到激励，以致于顺理成章，我们想到要出版其中一些成果。杨炼和我合作编辑了《玉梯》，这是一部近三十年来中文诗歌重要诗作的全面英译选本。编译这本书的理念，正是基于上述一系列诗歌节与交流活动的直接结果。

另外，我们也意识到，因为翻译过程是双向进行的，一本如《玉梯》那样的大型诗集并不能专门地聚焦于互译过程。所以我们决定，第二本独立的书籍是必要的：一本英中互译诗选，一本主要基于"诗人对诗人"的翻译方法的作品汇集。

这一方法当然是集多年实践发展而成。杨炼和其他中国作家翻译过斯洛文尼亚语和其它语种的诗歌。波丽和朱利安曾与阿拉伯及以色列作家进行过类似项目。我自己，也翻译过诸如保加利亚语、波斯语、立陶宛语、索马里语、及土耳其语的诗作。

"诗人对诗人"的翻译改变了我作为一名作家的实践方式；而作为一名学者，它也成为我的主要研究领域。我开始为了翻译而旅行，与不同的组织建立联系，诸如英国阿伯里斯特威斯的跨边界文学，爱丁堡的苏格兰诗歌图书馆，以及以伦敦为基地的诗歌翻译中心；我还与其他的译者合作，例如，琳达·法兰西、理查德·格温、马汀·欧文和佐伊·斯哥尔丁等。

但是，杨炼和我从来也没有忘记，在中、英文之间进行的翻译工作具有独一无二的意义，它贯穿了我们随后进行的其他翻译活动。

中英两种语言以及两种文化的鸿沟看起来十分宽阔——很明显，英文由一套拼音系统表征，其拼词法也在编码它的语言和文化史；阅读英文，就是通过回溯词源而深入时间层次。

同样醒目的是，中文数千个汉字，通过组合象形文字和词根，在空间上表达概念及其互动。相同的字符可被应用于很不同的词汇，发音也截然不同，却又保留大致相同的涵义。这一点，以及汉字很久以前即已定型的事实——虽然最近半个世纪经过大量改革和简化——使得汉字看起来简直不受时间影响。

两种文化之间的差别亦很显著：以英语为典型的西欧思维和美国文化，在其无法再续殖民之处，持续地带有经验论的色彩。它是外向的，个人主义的。与之相似，中国思想在传统上聚焦于现象，创造了一个封闭的，等级制的社会系统。在此系统中，中国俨然已经就是一个世界，完满于其自身。共产主义几乎打破了古典世界观的基础，却又从根本上传承了那一思想模式，并将之翻译为一套独特的政治和工业合成体；修辞上貌似矛盾，党和资本主义合二而一了。

相比英语文学，中国文学要远为古老和范围宽泛。今天的人们耳熟能详古典汉语诗作；但几乎无法想象他们的生活。感谢那些不变的汉字，今天每个人都能阅读唐朝或者宋朝的杰作，但是，甚至无人能完全确定它们的发音。

另一方面，英语文学通过其语言学以及文化形式的演化，显示出明确的阶段性；有规律地，它要求其自身被翻译成最新近的表达形式。以某种方式，它显现出易变、通晓、相对均等的特性，由此而具有一种灵活性，令它看起来能够吻合当下的要求。

无论如何，当我们共同坐下来逐字逐行地翻译，　我刚刚描绘过的那一系列鸿沟，导致了一些丰富和悖谬的情形发生。一方面，讨论语言的表层就有必要讨论语言的深度。另一方面，英语对音乐性的专注，及漫长历史中对不同形式的韵律的操作，联接上了中文对格式的热爱，及其许多世纪以来对典故的格式化处理。

英语对音乐性的历史化，接触到了汉字的概念化；英语有关诗意的观念，碰撞着中文截然不同的音乐调性。每种文化以各自不同的方式充分成熟，技巧性地与另一方匹配，并在目的论意义上互相反差。从热烈的讨论中，我们兴奋地意识到，有些什么事物出现了，且利害攸关。

2.

那么，何为"诗人对诗人"的方法，它又是如何在这八年来演化出这本诗集所包含的内容呢？具体说，这进程是如何引导重心的变化，令我们开始双向互译诗歌的呢？

这一方法的根源可回溯至庞德在《如何去阅读》一文中的一句话。以其典型的绝对风格，庞德说道：

拙于语言的人们所误解的另一点是，一个人并不需要学会一套完整的语言来理解某一首或某一些诗。能够透彻地理解一首诗，理解构成它的几十个或几百个字词中的每一个，这通常也就足够了。

那么，"诗人对诗人"的翻译，也就是一个诗人从作者可疑的权威位置上，告知另一位诗人那"几十个或几百个字词"的全面文化内涵。当一种共同语言（通常都是英语）被使用，运用这种对话进行翻译，并不需要事先准备好一个文本，逐字逐句阐释字面或字里行间的意义。

在一位口译者（通常是一位熟练的译者或诗人/译者）的陪同下，工作在诗人与诗人之间完成。有时候，当诗作者不能到场，译者诗人也可以和口译者工作。在后一种情况中，原作语言很可能被附加新的张力。译者应（也确有必要）不仅是一位文学翻译专家，而且能与诗作者密切联系，展开咨询去测定他们的反应。

后两种情况中，字面直译时有发生，使得翻译情形复杂化。我稍后会谈及此点。

然而，上述三种情况的目标一致：通过源语言和译文语言的作者之间富于活力的对话，创造出可以被出版的文本。在几个重要的方面，它改变了一般的翻译程序。

首先也最重要的，作品通常由原著者选择。这反转了通常由专业译者从外语诗歌原作中挑选作品的程序；也因此，它颠覆了以假想的翻译轻松程度、或为"适应"对象文化的意识形态或美学要求去选择诗作的秩序。很长时间以来，中文是一系列东方主义姿态的主题，上述方法对此予以反击。尽管我们能理解，这并不能完全地避开它们。这一程序有冒险性——人们或许会发现，一些作品几乎无法被有效翻译，或在译文中相对减弱了效力。它经常会显得比我们最初预料的难译得多。但，发现诗人认为哪些作品能代表自己所带来的益处，远甚于这些危险。

其二，原作者活跃的在场，或易于找到他们，有助于为待建构的译作提供更详尽、并（或可争辩地）更准确的图景。至少，它能暴露任何翻译程序都会有的大量第二手猜测。由于可以直接询问作者，译者考量意图与涵义、姿态与语调的层次也更清晰。

　　其三，一位诗人译者的在场，可能意味着一场有关形式问题的高水平讨论，其达成的共识，比双方在韵律，意象，及习语上各自雕琢的要多得多。事实上，"诗人对诗人"的方法，为在技巧水平上更强有力地处理文化翻译问题打开了空间。

　　以上三种肯定性因素能使原作诗人与诗人/译者共享反思。作为这一程序的一部分，向原作诗人的大量提问，并非是他在创作该诗篇时所想到过的。

　　同样，对译者，这一过程能迫使他们从一种更富批判性的外在角度反思自己的创作习惯与视点，并评估他自己是否确实能与目标保持一致。两位作家经常遭遇到这种情况：相同的文学技巧、方式，或参照系统，被他们附着上了不同的文化重量。

　　双方对各自诗歌创作步骤和创造力获得的意识角度（无论如何不全面）——可以被视为翻译过程的一种间接效果，但它对项目的成功极富含义。依赖双方超脱各自局限的能力，"诗人对诗人"对话模式带来、并确实导致了方法或实践上的变化。成功的翻译通常更取决于这种变化的实质，它远远超过双方所预期的。

　　这便是我们在标题"第三岸"中所指涉的处境；一片源语言或译文语言的诗歌习惯或文化潮流不能完全统辖的领地。

　　苏格兰诗人休·麦克迪尔米德不得不经常探讨那些不列颠诸岛不同语言间变幻莫测的跨越。在他的长诗《纪念詹姆士·乔伊斯》中，他尝试过一种既有关转换又有关翻译的表达——"他欢迎乔伊斯来到我们的AONACH"——他合成了两个盖尔语词汇：其一指聚会地点或市场，其二指山脊或高处。

　　他的诗《在高高升起的海滩上》中，第三岸作为诗人之间，诗作之间的对话点，得到了推论性的印证：数个代纪的地理变化真的把海岸提升到水面之上，滞留于海滩的石头，象征了一种诗人尝试用语言去企及的"无法被质疑的现实"。他采用了一种特别的，被极大拓展的科学语汇混合设得兰岛挪威语，试图将那些石头翻译成字词：

　　这只猫生命的摇篮；这易变却悬置未决的现实；
　　石头内一阵密集的震颤
　　使它们看上去静止不动......

这种诗行间，韵律上，意象里，语调中，字或词内潜藏的高密度冲突——足以表明其不可译——而这正是"诗人对诗人"翻译法铆定的目标。

　　或许，这种对话的强度本身，已包含着它失败的种子。对于被翻译的诗人来说，在重新思考他或她自己的作品时，存在一种诱惑，那便是，用翻译来发展某种被讨论中探索的观念，翻译成了修改的一种方式。对于译者诗人，存在着一种类似的诱惑：根据自己的直觉和原则来赋予诗歌含义，而不是耐心地通过探讨和反复润饰译稿来呈现原作文本的意义和风格。

对翻译稿和创作稿的流畅性的这种混淆，可能会导致某种"双人疯狂"（FOLIE À DEUX）。这就是为什么对话最好由一位译者主持，恰如一位婚姻顾问，这位译者能够在关键时刻将双方拉回到文本本身。这也是为什么当不止有一位译者诗人时，关于译文语言的风格和诠释问题的对话会更丰富。这样做的结果也许较少个人化，但也更能抵抗个人的习惯。

所以，理想的"诗人对诗人"翻译模式，是一种"四人对话"。它包括，其一，在场的或可接触到的原作者；其二，口译或中介诗人／译者；其三和其四，两位来自译文语言的诗人。当然，这四个角色可以由两方或三方来扮演，但四方的参与保证了最大程度的投入和客观性。

如上所述，起初，并没有任何其他文本可依据：两位诗人一同坐下来，他们拥有的只是源语言诗人挑选的一首诗，然后他们开始工作。逐渐地，某种直译形式所扮演的角色开始显得管用。但随即，也带来了它自身的危险。

自然，一首诗的字面含义使得工作可以开始。但字面含义，从来不止是它们自身。它们通常是具有其强烈美学原则（无论是否清晰地表达）的作者／译者的创造物。现在，他们不得不勉力向译者诗人（们）作出解释。此时，译者会占用这翻译法的相当一部分——尤其当原作者不在场、或他对译文语言通晓不畅时——去推测字面含义，而非致力于以理解原作为目标。

口译或直译阶段的作者，有可能不太能体会译者诗人不同工作阶段上的意义。有时，这一点也很难解释：直译译文在另外文化语境里也许不够出版水平。强调字典释义和对原作者亦步亦趋，也可能会造成一定障碍。

因此，在工作中，诗人们使用字面含义通常主要为了帮助选择，从而能够着手创造字里行间的意义——字面对字面的翻译，保留词序，列出同义词，关注随时产生的文化或风格问题。这种对字里行间意义的建构，明确地通过解构字面含义而达成，它会直接引发我上面讨论过的对话。

3.

我在为《玉梯》撰写的序言中，表达过我从编纂这本书的过程中获得的信念，那就是，翻译是任何对话过程的一个重要方面，而非仅是在不同语言之间传递意义。不同年代之间，不同阶级之间，不同性别之间，甚或从一种记忆到当下自我的世界观，都将我们纳入某种类型的翻译。

不言自明，这是对"翻译"一词的隐喻用法，但我们必须经常对这类隐喻保持敏感，通过它们，我们将此类交流观念化。许多我们有关翻译的隐喻倾向于等级论的假定，从带有性别色彩的"母语"，到意义可能会在传递中"流失"的观念，似乎意义是件行李——或商品。然而，存在一种更根本的意识，那就是，翻译自身就是隐喻性的；这一点，与本诗集汇集的诗人们所采用的方式和所作出的选择，有着直接的关系。

人们通常假定，译者以一种或可被称作转喻的方法来工作；当译者寻找语言，形式，意象或文化典故的对等表达，人们会猜想，他们将寻找相近的表达—— 同义词而非反义词，与原作字数相近的音节数，有相同参照系的意象，和看起来尽可能"接近"的文化对等物。

但常出现的情况却是，译者所寻找到是隐喻对等物 ——字词，韵律，意象，典故，他们与原作"相像"，却不一定要直接对应。这种相像性，恰如在隐喻当中，是由在目标语言中创造一首诗歌这一行动不言明地产生的。在某种意义上，翻译自身就是原作的隐喻。按I.A.理查德的话来说，原作是高音，翻译是为高音赋形的载体。

我认为，当我们关注中英文之间的互译，这种关系尤其清晰。汉语象形文字和涵义之间的动力通常是转喻的。例如，表示"新鲜的"（FRESH）这个汉字，"鲜"（拼音为"XIĀN"），包含了来自相邻近元素的一种联想 —— 它包含表示两样新鲜事物的字，"鱼"和"羊"（YÚ和YÁNG）.

相反，对于讲英语的人来说，"FRESH"凭借一个古英语的单音节词来传达联想。就是说，无论我们是否意识到其词源，大部分讲英语的人会注意到它发音的直接性，将它与含义相联系，却并不会直捷联想到"NEOTERIC"（"新颖的"）或者 "UNCONTAMINATED"（"未经污染的"）。英语中的同义词有其不同的来源，我们并不经常指认它们为相邻的，事实上，它们有可能被体验为明显差异的存在。

所以，当我们考虑"鲜"和"FRESH"的关系，我们在隐喻地思考，一种字符间的空间关系，如何能够通过互补或相对的语言学之根而建立一种相像的意义；也即，一种通过时间关系所建立的相像的意义。我相信，这也是中国诗人于坚最近在南京的一个诗歌节所讲的，"汉字无法被翻译。"他是指，翻译中文令我们横向地思考对等物本身。

认为翻译就像搜寻意义一样搜寻着隐喻，是要注意到，"相像性"（LIKENESS）与"相似性"（SIMILARITY）有着微妙的不同。一对双胞胎也许看上去与对方相差无几，却可能有着不同的内质。而两个陌生人或许在每个方面与对方相异，却可能承认——或至少认可 ——他们在某些方面基本上相像。

作为超越了对对方的语言和文化领会的极限的诗人，他们必须对对方的判断保持信念——这个意义上，仅仅当被译和译者诗人建立起信任以后，翻译才是从这一信念的起跳。那么，"诗人对诗人"的翻译，就不是一种万无一失的方法，而是一种关系，在这关系中，我们希望认可并且赋予"相像"以重要性。

这本书的形成过程中，对相像性的认可一再呈现。因为双方语言的诗人都认可，对方对各自文化的政治，历史和诗体学的参与，不仅只是与其自身相似,或不仅只是简单的平行操作,而是几乎同出一辙的投入。证据很简单,双方都会被对方与自己的作品的种种关联深深吸引。

当然,对于如下这一点,许多英国诗人反应颇为强烈:中国作家们通过对他们的古典遗产进行激进的探索来重构他们与先锋技巧(通常是从美国诗歌中引进的)的关系;在这种关系中,一方面,既不假定存在与那一遗产的简单、直接的关联;另一方面,经历了文化大革命的恐怖后,更不存在与那个过去的截然断裂 —— 这种断裂既不被认为是可取的,也不是可能的。我们中的一些人感到,与此不无相像的是,贯穿整个二十和二十一世纪的英国和爱尔兰诗歌创作,有关实验性和传统诗歌与诗学之间问题的讨论一直存在。对于中英诗人而言,拥有范围宽广、多种多样的形式资源和理论方法,具有同等重要的意义。

我们由此希望,使用一种如此强调对话的翻译方法,凭借我们所拥有的共享价值观和共同投入,可能缓解这类诗集对其内容及作者带来的约束力。

我们的文化并不具有视对方为一个当代实体的精细意识,尤其当它涉及到诗歌领域。因此,特别是对那些沉思中国文化广阔性的英语读者,也相对于那些虑及(从美国到英国到印度,澳大利亚等)英文多样性的中文读者而言,经常存在一种提喻法思维的诱惑———种以部分代表全体的修辞策略。"我才不会面面俱到地阅读呢,"他们想,即便在这个想法产生之后也拒绝承认。"所以,这首诗应该代表这位诗人;这位诗人应该代表那种文化运动;而这部诗集,应该足以整体地代表那种语言的诗歌。"

这本诗集同时在两个方向上运动,试图置换此种替代性的行为。一种语言为读者展示了它自身的一幅肖像,另一幅画像由对方选择的译文语言所提供。这两种形象同时鼓励着比较和对照。它们各自在对话,正如互译的诗人在对话。事实上,正如代表各自的文化那样,它们代表了那一过程,并暗示了某些局限性:这一类诗集只能包含每种文化中那准备好的、实际上能够参与此类对话的部分:还有许多其他部分没有、或不能这样做。

这正是那一类被许多作家认作巨大解放的局限性:技术限制为发明创造了条件,它使得你能够挣脱其他的,更为教条主义的约束。我认为,我们并不希望如提喻法阅读所暗示的那样,用一种直捷的方式去代表我们的文化。我们更希望去探索,作为从这类表现中解放出来的作家和译者,我们能做些什么;从而进入一个与对方,与我们自身,与对方读者以交流作为重要元素的区域。在那一区域,如果原作和译作的质量足够高,作者和读者将创造他们各自的理解,来理解我们各自的诗歌,它们的关联和对比,它们显明的特性与可能的普遍性。事实上,他们将在第三岸登陆。

(梁俪真 译)

中诗英译

Chinese into English

姜涛

空军一号

飞机穿越云层，带来列岛的焦虑
那些匍匐在海礁上
演习的官兵，才习惯了说hello
又要唐突地竖起自己
在灯火通明的冲绳县厅

可是你，"黑身体"的大统领
"黑身体"的大情人
今夜，又下榻在哪里？
隔壁，又睡了哪一位白身体的
照耀了亚洲事物的国务卿？

从太平洋暗流中，谁又能
慢慢游过来，露出
圆圆的带星星的军帽
敲敲你的腰，说：

"老兄！时候尚早
我们出去走走。"
2009.11.

Jiang Tao

Air Force One

The airplane cuts through thick clouds, bringing forth the archipelago's
        anxiety
Crawling on the reef, those soldiers
on military maneuvers just learned to say "hello"
Now they have to suddenly stand up
in the Okinawan town hall ablaze with lights
while you, President in a black body,
great lover of one black body,
tonight, where are you going to stay?
In bed next door, which Secretary of State, in white body, is it
that illuminates Asian affairs?
Out of the Pacific undercurrent, who can
swim slowly toward here, appearing
in a round cap with a single star,
and knocking on you, say,
"Buddy, it's still early,
let's go out for a walk."

(Translated by Arthur Sze)

冷霜

小夜曲
（为X·Y而作）

血在血管里流得多么慢
仿佛心脏已经是石头
露出水面的部分
长满了苔藓

停电了。一截短短的蜡烛
在纸面上放下一只桔子
颤抖的边缘
像黑暗的牙痛

此时，一扇失修的门
正在音乐厅里熟睡
并且，在人已走光的梦中
断断续续地，鼓着掌

我的手指触到的
是夜的残缺的、温暖的驼背
是另一方消失后的通话中
仍然竖着的那副听筒

Leng Shuang

Serenade
      (for X. Y.)

Blood flows so slowly in my veins
it seems my heart is already
a stone protruding from water,
covered over with moss.

A power outage. A candle stub
leaves a tangerine on the paper,
the edge shivering
like the twilight's toothache.

Now, an unrepaired door
falls asleep in the music hall
and in the dreams of those who've left,
an intermittent clapping.

What my fingers touch
is the night's incomplete, warm hunched back,
or the disappeared conversation
over the lifted receiver.

(Translated by Eleanor Goodman)

唐晓渡

五月的蔷薇
——致R·Y

当然，这是一个秘密——
缠绵的藤蔓
怎样从荆棘丛中
一把抓住春天

却不知怎么打开
就这么暗暗攥着
整整一个冬天的蓄积
憋得血管发蓝

迎春开过，樱花开过
然后是桃花、杏花
压缩再压缩的热情
竟会有雪花的冷淡

慢。必须是慢！
忍耐缓解着忍耐的负担
这世上不会有过时的芳香
看那些在风中晃动的小拳头

——我的花事，一百万颗
瞬时齐爆的集束炸弹！

2002.5.4.

Tang Xiaodu

May Rose
(for R.Y.)

Of course, this is a secret—
how the trysting vines
have snatched the spring
from the armoured branches

but, not knowing how to undress it,
clutch it with a secret strength
this way, the winter through,
tense the vines of themselves to blue.

While snowdrops bloom, then the cherry,
in turn the peach, the apricot,
this fervour keeps, buried and buried
to the indifference of snow.

Slowly! It must come slowly.
Endurance eases the weight of endurance.
No true fragrance will be too late in this world.
Look at these little fists mobbing the wind—

my flower affair like a million bombs
bursting all at once, at once.

(Translated by Antony Dunn)

镜
——给我的孩子

镜子挂在墙上
我们悬在镜中
毛茸茸的笑声把镜面擦了又擦
——"这是爸爸"
一根百合的手指探进明亮的虚空

一根百合的手指来自明亮的虚空
——"这是爸爸"
水银的笑声在心底镀了又镀
我们隐入墙内
镜子飞向空中

叫出你的名字

叫出你的名字
就是召唤月亮、星辰和大地
光流尽荒漠
桑田无边涌起
一只蚕蛹咬破茧壳
我叫出你的名字

叫出你的名字
就是召唤根、鲜花和果实
麦芒刺痛天空
云烟横布心事
一叶利刃滑过咽喉
我叫出你的名字

叫出你的名字
就是召唤风、波涛和神迹
落日挽紧帆篷
群鸟飞进海市
一块石头滚下山坡
我叫出你的名字

Mirror
(for my daughter)

A mirror hangs on a wall
and we're floating in its space
again and again this downy laughter brushes past:
'That's Daddy,'
a lily's finger pointing into hollow brightness.

The lily's finger pokes out of a hollow brightness:
'That's Daddy.'
Quicksilver laughter brushes the back of my heart
and we fade into the wall;
the mirror flies into space.

I cry out your name

crying out your name
invoking moon stars and earth
the light exhausts the wilderness
the cultivated field rises, endless
an immature silkworm bites through the cocoon
I cry out your name

crying out your name
invoking roots flowers and fruits
the ear of wheat pricks the sky
the bank of cloud permeates my knowing
a sharp blade strokes the throat
I cry out your name

crying out your name
invoking winds waves and miracles
the setting sun draws sails into an embrace
the flock of birds flies into a mirage
one rock rolls down the slope
I cry out your name

叫出你的名字
就是召唤我自己
帷幔次第拉开
玻璃澄清墙壁
唯一的钥匙折断锁孔
我只好沉默。只好让沉默

叫出
叫出你的名字

无题

递你一支烟
连同我的臂膀
连同火竖在我掌心的波浪
燃烧的唇线比黑暗更锋利
"女人抽烟不好"
——我刚想开口
夜已被隐隐灼伤

警灯闪亮
谁会把一生叼在嘴上
呼——吸——呼——吸
呼吸 呼吸 呼吸
呼吸呼吸呼吸呼吸
红 更红 再红些
——就这样！必须这样！只能这样！

晨曦微茫
夜在墙角脱下黑色的大氅
远处有雄鸡在试着打鸣
身边有人耳语：光！
呵，更多的光！

而那些吸剩的烟头听不见
它们埋在灰烬里一声不响
苍白 冷淡 深刻
比烟缸更是烟缸

crying out your name
invoking myself
the velvet curtain opens fold upon fold
the panes make the wall transparent
one unique key breaks the lock
I have to be silent. Let the silence

cry out
cry out your name

Untitled

All at once you get the offer of
a cigarette, my shoulder
and the figure of this flame, out of my grasp, leaving a trace like a wave
it makes the outline of your lips burn, sharper than the darkness—
I want to open my mouth, tell you
'It's not good for women to smoke'
but the night is already very slightly burnt

A police siren flickers
Who'd let his entire life dangle from his lips like this?
in—hale—ex—hale
inhale exhale inhale
exhalinhalexhalinhale
red   redder   redder still
It's exactly like this. It has to and could only be like this.

Morning comes, unclear
night takes off its long black coat in a corner by the wall
in the distance roosters are trying to crow
to one side someone whispers, 'Light!'
sighs, 'More light!'

But the smoked-down remains of cigarettes can't hear
buried in the ashes without a sound
colourless   cold   sunk
If an ashtray can mean something, then they mean something more

(Translated by W.N. Herbert)

无题（之三）

愤怒的柳树把春天扯成棉絮
玫瑰在咆哮。灰烬喷吐着新意
当然火焰有可能熄灭于半空
但落地之前
谁曾对你说，我将离去！

我将离去……
我又能去往哪里？
在刀锋上跳舞
我的脚早已鲜血淋漓
白的血。白白的血
瑜伽功教我向上腾跃
我上不着天，下不着地

这就是罪！
是前世就已挖成陷阱的罪
因无辜而格外残忍
谁不服，谁就越陷越深
黑水晶面对铁锤必须绽开微笑
我说过，我罪孽深重

这是唯一的真实。其余都是谎言
但真实的谎言比铁锤更令人动容
你看它步步生莲，旋舞得有多精彩
如同我梦幻般悬在空中
跺脚、叹气、抓耳挠腮
像一个幕间小丑
和哈哈大笑的观众一起
对着自己起哄——

是的，这就是罪
是不服不行的罪！
谁能测出从玫瑰到刀锋的距离？
在灰烬中跳舞

我哪儿都不去！

3ʳᵈ part of an untitled poem

Furious willows tear the spring into cotton fluff,
roses roar, and ash trees push out new meaning
Of course the flame can be made out, but only in mid-air
before it comes down to ground
Who told you I would leave?

I would leave…
but where else could I go?
Dancing on a blade
my feet are already bleeding
white blood, blank blood
Yoga teaches me to jump—
I can reach neither heaven nor earth

This is sin:
sin built into a trap within four generations
Even more cruel: whoever refuses out of innocence
will be even more profoundly trapped
The black crystal must smile when it faces the iron hammer
I said, I am profoundly unequal

This is the only truth   All others are lies—
but true lies are more transformative than iron hammers
Look at the lotus growing in your every footstep
How wonderful the whirling dance is,
as if I float in mid-air like a dream
tapping, sighing, tugging my ears and scratching at my cheeks
like the interval clown
with his uproarious audience—
making trouble for myself

Yes, this is sin:
sin you have to submit to
Who can measure the distance between the roses and the blades?
Dancing in the ashes

I'm not going anywhere

(Translated by Fiona Sampson)

王小妮

一块布的背叛

我没有想到
把玻璃擦净以后
全世界立刻渗透进来。
最后的遮挡跟着水走了
连树叶也为今后的窥视
纹浓了眉线。
我完全没有想到
只是两个小时和一块布
劳动,居然也能犯下大错。
什么东西都精通背叛。
这最古老的手艺
轻易地通过了一块柔软的脏布。
现在我被困在它的暴露之中。
别人最大的自由
是看的自由。
在这个复杂又明媚的春天
立体主义走下画布。
每一个人都获得了剖开障碍的神力
我的日子正被一层层看穿。
躲在家的最深处
却袒露在四壁以外的人
我只是裸露无遗的物体。
一张横竖交错的桃木椅子
我藏在木条之内
心思走动。
世上应该突然大降尘土
我宁愿退回到
那桃木的种子之核。
只有人才要隐秘
除了人
现在我什么都想冒充。

Wang Xiaoni

Betraying Cloth

I never thought
the world would creep in
after I washed the window.
Now the grime is washed away
even the leaves spy on me.

I never thought
a cloth and two hours
of scrubbing could be such a crime.

Everything is betrayal—
this ancient art
is easily passed through a soft rag
and now I'm snared in its mesh.

The greatest freedom
is to see.
In this shifting and radiant spring
people's distorted faces slide past the pane.
Each has the power to break through.
My days are peeled off layer by layer

until I'm stripped to the bone.
I hide as my thoughts spin
inside the bars of a peachwood chair.

Dust must shroud the earth.
I would rather become
a peach stone.

Only people need secrecy.
I want to be anything
but human.

(Translated by Pascale Petit)

台风四首

1. 今天满天的风

海岛竖起来
全身的羽毛都兴奋。
威力倾斜着从海那边跳舞过来
玻璃在咬牙。

一直一直一直
什么都做不下去。
站着,看今天的风
看这成群的流寇中,夹带一个或两个灰怆的英雄。

2. 晾晒在强风中的一列男装

是谁家的儿子,谁家的西风。
那队士兵在一截铁丝上急行军
椰树在四周爆破,隔一会儿一只红椰落地。

不知道为什么就十万火急的下午
无礼的风窜上海岛,驱赶着那无辜的队伍。
在两棵苍老的紫荆中间
抽打他们的上半身。

前心紧贴着后背
风的队列里,人人都是空的。

3. 台风来临的晚上

台风之夜,天空满了,人间被扫荡。

从西向东,成群的黑牛在头顶上打滚
风的蹄子一遍一遍捣窗
地上的一切都要升天了。

Four Typhoon Poems

1. Today the Wind Invaded the Sky

The island stood up—
all its body feathers were excited.
The cyclone leaned forward and danced from the other side of the sea.
The windowpanes gnashed their teeth.

I stood and stood—
I could not do anything.
I stood looking at today's wind,
watched the rampaging bandits carry their few pathetic grey heroes.

2. A Line of Jackets Airing in the Gale

Whose son do these belong to? Whose west wind
is quick-marching that troop of soldiers on the washing-line,
coconut trees blasting all around them, red coconuts crashing every few
　　　seconds?

Nobody knows why the rude wind rushed onto our island
on such an urgent afternoon and drove these innocent soldiers
between two old bauhinia trees,
beating their torsos—

the fronts of their jackets sticking to the backs.
In the gale's army, every uniform was empty.

3. The Evening the Typhoon Arrived

On the evening of the typhoon, the sky filled up, the human world was
　　　wiped clean.

From west to east, herds of black bulls stampeded overhead.
The gale's hooves kept knocking against the windows.
Everything on earth rose up to heaven.

人装在夜里
夜晚装在正爆开的鼓里。
狂妄的气流
从另外的世界推出滚滚战车。
没见到丝毫的抵抗
了不起的事情就都是这样发生的。

4. 结局出现了

植物割断了长发
遍地跳着来不及死去的神经
疯子撞破了疯人院
终于轮到疯子们庆贺胜利了。

我在鱼肚子里坐稳
满心的颠簸，满心跑着大云彩。

天堂拔出电的鞭子。
风雨压扁了城市
刮尽它新贴上去的那层浮光闪烁的金鳞。
得意的人们转眼就败下去
昨天还在窗前的膨胀荷塘，一下子矮多了。
躲在深处那人，看看这结局吧。

Humans were enclosed by the evening,
the evening was enclosed in a blasting drum.
Arrogant gusts

rolled out chariots from the otherworld
and didn't meet any resistance.
This is how these things happened.

4. THE AFTERMATH

Plants had their long hair sheared,
any nerves that had not yet died writhed over the ground.
Lunatics smashed their asylums—
at last it was their turn to party.

I sat safe in a fish's belly.
My heart heaved with huge dark yellow clouds.

Heaven unleashed whips of lightning.
Wind and rain crushed the city,
scratched off its newly painted gold scales.
The swollen lotus pond in front of the window suddenly shrivelled.
The puffed-up were ruined in an instant.

(Translated by Pascale Petit)

在威尔士（选三）

1. 端起牛奶的孩子

那男孩端不动那大瓶牛奶。
正像一小块土地不可能去举起海
但是他要试试。

用力捧着那白的圣物
想把它放平在古老的木桌上
把这个圣物放在另一个圣物之上。

牛奶是白的，桌面是黑的
孩子的两只手有十根光洁的指头
这世上的圣物并不都一样。

我看见那男孩动作中的幸福，就不敢再往深想了。

2. 一头牛

一头黑牛走近，想让我看看它那身锦缎
走得比哪位皇帝都慢
穿过早雾的帘子，从它独居的绿宫殿里。

看我的时候，它只用一只眼
另一只眼搜寻着雾的边缘
那儿有它的卫队。
我觉得它大约是东方的某位皇帝
穿着上好的香云沙
我在1000年前见过他。

from **Wales in June**

1. A Boy Holding a Milk Bottle

That boy could not hold up the big milk-bottle
just as a small patch of land can't hold up the sea.
But he wanted to try,

he held that white liquid with all his strength.
He wanted to place it on the old wooden table,
place this sacred object on another sacred object.

The milk was very white; the tabletop was black,
the boy's hands had ten clean and shining fingers.
The sacred objects of this world—you turned out in different forms.

Looking at the boy drinking milk, face-upwards, I dared not think any
    deeper.

2. A Bull

A black bull approached me, wanting to show off his silky fur
so he walked slower than an emperor in any dynasty.
Emerging from the blinds of morning fog, he came out of his green palace.

When he looked at me it was only with one eye,
the other was searching the edge of the fog
where his armed escort was waiting in ambush.
Possibly, he was an oriental emperor
wearing best quality Xiang Yun silk.
I've seen this same carefree gaze
a thousand years ago.

(Translated by Pascale Petit)

月光白得很

月亮在深夜照出了一切的骨头。
我呼进了青白的气息。
人间的琐碎皮毛
变成下坠的萤火虫。
城市是一具死去的骨架。
没有哪个生命
配得上这样纯的夜色。
打开窗帘
天地正在眼前交接白银
月光使我忘记我是一个人。
生命的最后一幕
在一片素色里静静地彩排。
月光来到地板上
我的两只脚已经预先白了

White Moon

The midnight moon exposes every bone.

I breathe ice-blue air.
All the world's follies
are falling like fireflies.
The city is a carcass.

No living thing
can match this pure light.
I open the curtains to watch earth
hold such pouring silver
until I forget I'm human.

Life's last act
is silently rehearsed under a bleak spotlight.
The moon lands on my floor
to reveal my blanched feet.

(Translated by Pascale Petit)

西川

巨兽

那巨兽，我看见了。那巨兽，毛发粗硬，牙齿锋利，双眼几乎失明。那巨兽，喘着粗气，嘟囔着厄运，而脚下没有声响。那巨兽，缺乏幽默感，像竭力掩盖其贫贱出身的人，像被使命所毁掉的人，没有摇篮可资回忆，没有目的地可资向往，没有足够的谎言来为自我辩护。它拍打树干，收集婴儿；它活着，像一块岩石，死去，像一场雪崩。

乌鸦在稻草人中间寻找同伙。

那巨兽，痛恨我的发型，痛恨我的气味，痛恨我的遗憾和拘谨。一句话，痛恨我把幸福打扮得珠光宝气。它挤进我的房门，命令我站立在墙角，不由分说坐垮我的椅子，打碎我的镜子，撕烂我的窗帘和一切属于我个人的灵魂屏障。我哀求它："在我口渴的时候别拿走我的茶杯！"它就地掘出泉水，算是对我的回答。

一吨鹦鹉，一吨鹦鹉的废话！

我们称老虎为"老虎"，我们称毛驴为"毛驴"。而那巨兽，你管它叫什么？ 没有名字，那巨兽的肉体和阴影便模糊一片，你便难以呼唤它，你便难以确定它在阳光下的位置并预卜它的吉凶。应该给它一个名字，比如"哀愁"或者"羞涩，应该给它一片饮水的池塘，应该给它一间避雨的屋舍。没有名字的巨兽是可怕的。

一只画眉把国王的爪牙全干掉！

它也受到诱惑，但不是王宫，不是美女，也不是一顿丰饶的烛光晚宴。它朝我们走来，难道我们身上有令它垂涎欲滴的东西？ 难道它要从我们身上啜饮空虚？ 这是怎样的诱惑呵!侧身于阴影的过道，迎面撞上刀光，一点点伤害使它学会了的呻吟——呻吟，生存，不知信仰为何物；可一旦它安静下来，便又听见芝麻拔节的声音，便又闻到月季的芳香。

飞越千山的大雁，羞于谈论自己。

这比喻的巨兽走下山坡，采摘花朵，在河边照见自己的面影，内心疑惑这是谁；然后泅水渡河，登岸，回望河上雾霭，无所发现亦无所理解；然后闯进城市，追踪少女，得到一块肉，在屋檐下过夜，梦见一座村庄、一位伴侣；然后梦游五十里，不知道害怕，在清晨的阳光里

Xi Chuan

Monster

I see it coming, panting with bad news,
ashamed of where it's been and what it brings
and how it somehow can't recall a thing.
It gathers us up, quietly, by ones, by twos,
avalanching into town—somewhere new
to find someone to get its teeth into—

> *Hell, I feel like a bird looking for a flock*
> *in a field of scarecrows…*

It hates me, for sure, from haircut to heart—
the mourning, the caution and all that broods
in the fakery of my lighter moods.
It'll squeeze through this dead-locked door and start
to smash up me place from mirrors to blinds;
all the stuff to stuff a life behind—

> *Listen to me; I'm spouting guano here—*
> *a sea of guano…*

Let's call a spade a spade to give ourselves
a handle on the thing—without a name
the monster's fleshed and dressed in mist—and tame
the cloud of it until the dark resolves
to something we can get our heads around:
the dread of all we love gone underground—

> *Fuck, what if I'm the cock clawing his bloody life out*
> *from under a pit of beaten friends…*

Our monster will not have you turn its head
with all your bling—it couldn't give a squib
for your ride, your chick, your million-dollar crib,
your politics, your place, your faith, your bed
of stinking roses—it's locked onto that bit
that knows even a vacuum can turn to shit—

醒来，发现回到了早先出发的地点：还是那厚厚的一层树叶，树叶下面还藏着那把匕首——有什么事情要发生？

沙土中的鸽子，你由于血光而觉悟。
啊，飞翔的时代来临了！

我奶奶

我奶奶咳嗽，唤醒一千只公鸡。
一千只公鸡啼鸣，唤醒一万个人。
一万个人走出村庄，村庄里的公鸡依然在啼鸣。
公鸡的啼鸣停止了，我奶奶依然在咳嗽。
依然在咳嗽的我奶奶讲起他的奶奶，声音越来越小。
仿佛是我奶奶的奶奶声音越来越小。
我奶奶讲着讲着就不讲了，就闭上了眼睛。
仿佛是我奶奶的奶奶到这时才真正死去。

奶奶

院子。五百年的历史。她见证了其中的九十六年。她坐在西厢房内的小竹椅上梳着头，梳着头。门开着。她的侧面。在她周围，是灶台、灶台上的锅、桌子、桌子上的酱油瓶、塑料篮子、篮中的白菜和胡萝卜，还有墙角的柴火。西厢房的屋顶上白云悠悠。西厢房内烟熏火燎，像一件被穿过九十六年不曾洗过的黑棉袄。九十六年把她变成一块遭逢了大旱的土地，只有她的眼睛湿润，湿润而浑浊，仿佛尚未完全枯干的水井。九十六年使她深陷在自己的身体里。亲人们俱已变作鬼魂。她仿佛是代表鬼魂活在这西厢房里。她那当过国民党营长的丈夫早已埋在共产党的青山之下。她梳着头，梳着头，一丝不苟。她已不再害怕将这简单的动做一遍遍重复。她已退到生活的底线，甚至低

Oh, somebody, please, give me wings to put a thousand miles between me and all this squawking about myself...

The poor creature wouldn't know its own face
in a mirror shop. It follows you, lost
as a lover, then eats you for breakfast.
Over and over it wakes to the taste
of the bender, the binge it's forgotten.
Hair of the dog. Sleep-walk. Again. Again—

Come on, you chicken—get some Tiananmen blood in you. Get on with it.

(Translated by Antony Dunn)

My Grandma

My grandma coughed, and woke up one thousand roosters.
A thousand roosters crowed and woke up ten thousand people.
Ten thousand people walked out of the village, the roosters still crowing.
Then the roosters' crowing stopped, but my grandma still coughed.
My grandma, still coughing, talked about her grandma, her voice
        growing dimmer and dimmer
as if my grandma's grandma's voice was growing dimmer and dimmer.
My grandma talked and talked and then stopped, and closed her eyes
as if my grandma's grandma actually died at that moment.

Grandma

Courtyard. A five hundred year history. She witnesses ninety six of these. She sits on a small bamboo chair in the west wing combing and combing her hair.

The open door. Her profile. Around her, a brick stove, the pot on the stove, a table, a bottle of soy sauce on the table, a plastic basket, cabbage and carrot in the basket,

firewood in the corner. Above the roof of the west wing are white clouds. Beneath the roof of the west wing are smoke-darkened walls

于这底线。她的脏布鞋踩到了比地面还低的地面。她梳着头,梳着头,认真得毫无道理,毫无意义。而花开在门外。当年的花呀……

佩玲

后来我知道她叫佩玲。
后来她回学校午休,我则继续在街头游逛。
我们是不约而同来到甘蔗摊旁。
我们一大一小两个人,一起嚼甘蔗,
一起将嚼干的甘蔗肉吐在地上,
一起看苍蝇飞来——原来苍蝇也喜欢甜味呵。
然后我们一起吃米粉,一起吃汤圆,
然后这小镇上最美的小女生问我来自什么地方。
我愿她快快长大,长成我暮年的女朋友。

like a black cotton padded coat that hasn't been washed for ninety six
years. Ninety six years have turned her into a piece of land stricken by a
long drought,

only her eyes are wet, wet and opaque, like a well that isn't totally dry.
Ninety six years have made her sink into her body.

All her relatives have become ghosts. As if she was living in the
west wing as the ghosts' representative. Her husband, who was a
Kuomintang battalion commander,

was buried many years ago in the Communists' green mountains. She
combs and combs her hair, meticulously, no longer afraid of repeating
this simple gesture

over and over again. She has retreated to the bottom line of life, to even
lower than this bottom line. Her dirty shoes have stamped the ground
even lower than the ground.

She combs and combs, carefully so as to lack meaning, and the flowers
are outside the door. She is the flower of those years...

Pei Ling

Later I got to know her name: Pei Ling.
Later she went back to her school to have a nap,
          and I kept on strolling down the street.
We had gone to the sugarcane stall as though by prior agreement.
The two of us, one big one small, together we chewed sugarcane,
together spat the husk of the sugarcane onto the ground
together saw the flies come—
          it turns out that flies are fond of sweet things too.
Then together we ate rice noodles, together ate rice balls,
then the most beautiful schoolgirl in this small town
          asked me where I came from.
I hope she grows up quickly so she can be my girlfriend
          in my old age.

(Translated by W.N. Herbert)

皮肤颂

枕头的褶皱压在皮肤上。小虫子的小爪子在皮肤上留下印迹。拔火罐从皮肤之下拔出血点。有毒的血点。

皮肤。我寂静的表层。我这不曾遭受过酷刑的皮肤,幻想着酷刑,就进入了历史,就长出了寂静的庄稼:我这了无历史感的汗毛。

山水画在皮肤上。地图刺在皮肤上。纳粹的人皮灯罩。乔叟时代英格兰的图书封皮用少女乳房的皮肤制成。

沙发,以牛皮为自己的皮肤,却不具有那死去动物的灵魂。每一次从牛皮沙发上站起,我总是忍不住牛鸣三声。

她的皮肤遇到了花朵:杨玉环。她的皮肤遇到了冰:王昭君。那些我永远无法遇到的皮肤,我只是说说而已。

但当我注目我潜伏着血管的皮肤,我也就看见了你清凉在夏季的皮肤。但我还想看见你的骨头。

无耻的骨头,裹着雅洁的皮肤,遇到什么样的皮肤它就会瞬间变得像骨头一样无耻?只有面颊懂得害羞和尴尬。

放大镜下皮肤的纹理。穿衣镜中皮肤的灰暗。麻子、痦子、疣子、鸡皮疙瘩。皮肤只将命运表达给能够读懂命运的人。

我的皮肤内装着我的疾病、快乐和幽暗。我的幽暗是灯光不能照亮的。

永久的七窍。临时性伤口。疼的皮肤。藏起来的皮肤。长在里面的皮肤。失去神经末梢的皮肤。死人的皮肤。

据说鬼魂没有皮肤也东游西逛。

据说太空人用皮肤来思想。

你用皮肤向我靠近,或者我用皮肤感受你的颤抖。我说不准你是否想要揭下我的皮肤去披到狼或者羊的身上。

Ode to Skin

Pillow creases on skin. The tiny feet of insects have left their prints—poisonous bloodspots medicinally sucked out.

Skin—my silent surface. This skin of mine has never experienced frenzied torture so it dreams of frenzied torture and thus slips into history. Then grows a silent crop: hairs without a sense of history.

Landscapes on skin. Maps with pins. A Nazi lampshade made of human skin. English books bound from girls' breasts in Chaucer's time.

A leather sofa doesn't have the dead cow's soul. But each time I get up from it I can't help mooing three times.

Consort Yang Yuhuan's skin touched flowers. Concubine Wang Zhaojun's skin touched ice. I have never met these skins so can only talk about them.

When I stare at my skin with its buried veins I also see your skin in a cool summer but can't see your bones.

Shameless bones coated with graceful skin. What makes graceful skin shameless as bones? Only cheeks get shy and embarrassed.

Skin lines under a magnifying glass. Skin's greyness in the wardrobe mirror. Pockmarks, blackheads, freckles, goose bumps. Skin only speaks to those who read fortunes.

My skin contains my sickness, happiness and my darkness, which can't be illuminated by any light.

I have seven perpetual gates and temporary wounds. Sore skin and dead skin without nerve tips, corpse-skin. It's said that ghosts wander without skins. It's said that aliens think with their skins.

You approach me with your skin, or my skin can feel yours shivering. I'm not sure whether you want to flay me and put my skin on a sheep or a wolf.

(Translated by Pascale Petit)

题王希孟青绿山水长卷《千里江山图》

绿色和蓝色汇集成空山。有人行走其间，但依然是空山，就像行走的人没有面孔，但依然是人。谁也别想从这些小人儿身上认出自己，就像世间的真山真水，别想从王希孟那里得到敷衍了事的赞扬。王希孟认识这些画面上的小人儿，但没有一个是他自己。这些不是他自己的小人儿，没有一个他能叫出名字。小人儿们得到山，得到水，就像山得到绿松石和青金石，水得到浩淼和船只，就像宋徽宗得到十八岁的王希孟，只是不知道他将在画完《千里江山图》之后不久便会死去。山水无名。王希孟明白，无名的人物，更只是山水的点缀，就像飞鸟明白，自己在人类的游戏中可有可无。鸟儿在空中相见。与此同时，行走在山间的人各有各的方向，各有各的打算。这些小人儿穿着白衣，行走，闲坐，打鱼，贩运，四周是绿色和蓝色，就像今天的人们穿着黑衣，出现在宴会、音乐会和葬礼之上，四周是金色和金色。这些白衣小人儿从未出生，当然也就从未死去，就像王希孟这免于污染和侵略的山水乌托邦，经得起细细的品读。远离桎梏的人呵谈不上对自由的向往，未遭经验损毁的人呵谈不上遗忘。王希孟让打鱼的人有打不尽的鱼，让山坳里流出流不尽的水。在他看来，幸福，就是财富的多寡恰到好处，让人们得以在山水之间静悄悄地架桥，架水车，修路，盖房屋，然后静悄悄地居住，就像树木恰到好处地生长在山岗、水畔，或环绕着村落，环绕着人。远景中，树木像花儿一样。它们轻轻摇晃，就是清风送爽的时候。清风送爽，就是有人歌唱的时候。有人歌唱，就是空山成其为空山的时候。

After Wang Ximeng's Blue and Green Horizontal Landscape Scroll, *A Thousand Miles of Rivers and Mountains*

Green colors and blue colors flow together and form empty mountains. Some people are walking in them, but they're still empty mountains, as if the people walking there have no faces, but they are still people. No one should try to recognize themselves in these figures, or try to see the real mountains and waters of this world, nor should anyone think of trying to gain casual praise from Wang Ximeng. Wang Ximeng knows these small figures, and that not one is he himself. These are not his figures, and he cannot call out a single one by name. The figures acquire the mountains and waters, just as the mountains acquire the emerald and lapis, just as the waters acquire vastness and boats, just as Emperor Huizong got Wang Ximeng at eighteen years old, not knowing that Wang would die soon after he finished this thousand miles of rivers and mountains. The mountains and waters are nameless. Wang Ximeng realizes that people without names are just decorations in mountains and waters, just as flying birds know they are insignificant to men's games. And the birds meet in the sky. Meanwhile, people walking in the mountains have their own directions to travel and their own plans. These small figures, in white, walk, sit at leisure, go fishing, trade, surrounded by green colors and blue colors, just like, today, people, in black, go to banquets, concerts, and funerals, surrounded by golden colors and more golden colors. These small figures in white have never been born and so have never died; just like Wang Ximeng's landscape utopia, they are immune to pollution and invasion, and that is worth careful consideration. So people who are far away from social controls have no need to long for freedom, and people who haven't been destroyed by experience aren't concerned about forgetting. Wang Ximeng let the fishermen have infinite numbers of fishes to go fishing; he allowed limitless waters to run out from the mountains. According to him, happiness means the exact amount of blessing so that, immersed in the silence between mountains and waters, people can build bridges, waterwheels, roads, houses, and live quietly, just like the trees growing appropriately in the mountains, along the margins of water, or surrounding a village, and surrounding people. In the distance, the trees are like flowers. When they sway, it's the time when the clear wind is rising. When the clear wind is rising, it's time for people to sing. When people sing, it's time for an empty mountain to become an empty mountain.

(Translated by Arthur Sze)

萧开愚

留赠拉斐尔

搬回温特土尔八年，成就很大，
买了住宅，到处是窗子、柜子，
抽屉多，配合你们的多语种吧，
备用的，藏着太久也就忘记了；
最大的建设是两个孩子，她们，
在地上要玩几年直到不好意思。
丁娜何必后悔呢，工作当旅游，
把可怜的申辩翻成定性的证据，
虽然，帮助的未必是什么好人；
富裕时间最好，把菜谱变成菜。
拉斐尔有点麻烦，从图书馆回
到书房，看见尽是古代的漂亮，
看窗外，对楼窗里的三个女孩
常常只穿内裤活动，干扰思想，
思想转弯，迂回在汉语的迷廊。
谜团吗，你要就有，正如猜想，
正如坐着埋头写文章，多无聊，
为幽深的书店，花匠般的店员，
更别说图书馆深山般的珍籍部，
你一定要雕琢一个像样的句子，
叨光以至于留宿。幸运挡不住，
像环扣，楼边的小溪流得清秀，
白天不听起夜听，叫愚溪正好。

2008，11月13日于温特土尔

Xiao Kaiyu

A Gift of Words for Raffael Keller

Moved back to Winterthur, after eight years of achievement
Bought an apartment, full of windows, sideboards, closets
Endless chests of drawers, as many as his languages,
Some kept in reserve so long, they've been quite forgotten;
The major work however, production of two daughters
Who run around so much they're certain to fall over.
Why then should Tina, have to work and travel
From courthouse to courthouse, talking and translating
For illegal immigrants who may well be criminals?
Let her have her holidays when she can try out recipes.
Raffael is troubled, returning from the library
Back from his study of ancient abstract beauty,
He spots three young women in the facing building
Who prove a sore distraction, wearing only panties.
His thoughts are revolving round mysterious corridors:
Chinese matters. Puzzled? Then carry on guessing,
Head buried deep in books. It's heavy work preparing
A sentence good enough for the deep dark library,
And the keeper of the books, not to mention pleasing
The higher echelons of Asian Rare Manuscripts,
With one sentence worthy to survive once you have vanished.
There are links of fortune that can't be simply broken.
The stream beside the house flows like a young maiden
You can't hear by night but only in the night-time
When you make your ablutions and recall the little streamlet
That is fit to be called *yu*: *yu*, the term of modesty,
Liu Zongyuan's stream, your study, and just *yu*.

(Translated by George Szirtes)

一次抵制

当几个车站扮演了几个省份，
大地好像寂寞的果皮，某种酝酿，
你经过更好的冒充，一些忍耐，
迎接的仅仅是英俊的假设。

经过提速，我来得早了，
还是不够匹配你的依然先进，依然突兀，
甚至决断，反而纵容了我的加倍的迟钝。

这果核般的地点也是从车窗扔下，
像草率、误解、易于忽略的装置，
不够酸楚，但可以期待。
因为必须的未来是公式挥泪。

我知道，一切意外都源于各就各位，
任何周密，任何疏漏，都是匠心越轨，
不过，操纵不如窥视，局部依靠阻止。

二〇〇五，十一月十八日，车过山东的时候

One Resistance

When several railways stations represent several provinces
The land's like piece of peel, waiting to be perfected
With a little endurance, with better disguise,
You welcome nothing but a handsome supposition.

As the train speeds up I arrive ahead of schedule,
But you are so far ahead, so abrupt I can't match you:
Even decisiveness indulges my double inertia.

The place is like a careless misunderstood ignored item of equipment.
Like an apple core thrown from the train window
Neither sour nor bitter enough, but not unexpected.
Because the assured future is formed to shed its tears.

I know all accidents are the result of some arrangement,
All schedules, all improvisations well-designed transgressions,
But to see a part is better than to control; part depends on impediment.

(Translated by George Szirtes)

山坡

开满野花,浮现在这个夜晚的
黑色砂纸上,白色的,黄色的
摇晃在吹拂而来的雾岚里,

鲜艳透明的水彩吹拂而来,
鸟儿们带来了单调的晚会,
在风景画中演奏,呵,二胡声音沙哑,

这样的安魂曲会把她吵醒,
从野花的压迫下站起,站起,
走回被遗忘占领的空间,

修辞学换掉了几批嘴巴的客厅,
饥饿术换掉了几道菜谱的厨房,
道德课换掉了几打内裤的卧室,

她将重新携带宽容的沉默
来到这个葱翠然而仿佛在移动的
篱笆旁边,脸庞绽露痛苦的笑容?

山坡的地下潮湿是地球在出汗,
野花的根在骨腔里蠕动,这些蛆虫
爬行为了吃掉我们最后依仗的坚硬。

表面上是死者继续作出牺牲,
其实是生者再一次死去,
这就是美好的体制转换。

请你回到山坡冰冷的汗液
和松弛的没有知觉的自我控制中间,
反而可以作出判断而不仅仅是忍受。

Hillside

Wildflowers cover the hillside, float
on the black sandpaper of this night—whites, yellows,
swirl in the blown mist,

fresh washes of colour drift in, mingle
with the dull chirp of birds in an unreal watercolour—
ah, the hoarse strains of the *erhu*,

such a requiem might wake her,
with the weight of the weeds, she stands up, stands up
and returns to the forgetting room.

In the sitting room, rhetoric has altered mouths,
in the kitchen, the art of hunger has altered menus,
in the bedroom, morality lessons have altered the underwear.

Will she return to the green shifting
hedge, with her stoic silence,
an agonised smile on her face?

Under the hill, the earth sweats,
roots worm through marrow, their maggot-tips
crawl to devour the last vertebra. I depend on these bones.

Apparently, the dead keep sacrificing themselves
but it's the living who do the dying—
this is the perfect reversal of systems.

Please—go back to the icy sweat of the hillside
and to the loose, automatic self-control
so that you can choose rather than endure.

(Translated by Pascale Petit)

严力

中国抽屉

我拉开一个个抽屉
翻阅自己经历过的岁月
抽屉里那些
曾经提心吊胆的地下诗稿
如今安静得能听见
养老的声音

抽屉里
还有一叠已成为古迹的粮票
自从它们成为古迹的那一天起
我就知道虽然它被称作了文物
但绝不为这块土地上的农作物
感到一丝骄傲

抽屉里
还有两枚红卫兵袖章
一枚已生锈的半钢手表
几张一九七六年四月五号
天安门悼念活动的现场照片
它们具有同样牺牲后的肃穆

抽屉啊中国抽屉
甚至在黑五类肉体上
拉开的抽屉里
也必会有一本红宝书

Yan Li

The Chinese Drawers

I pull out the Chinese drawers, one by one,
take a look at the years that I lived through;
in one drawer, those texts of
underground poems used to wrench themselves;
now, in the quiet, I can hear
the sounds of their retirement.

In another drawer
are a few grain coupons which are already antiques;
from the day they became obsolete,
I knew, even though they were cultural treasures,
they never had pride
for these crops from this land.

In another drawer
are two Red Guard bands,
one rusty fifty-per-cent steel watch,
and a couple of photos from the April 5, 1976
memorial in Tiananmen Square—
they all have the somber quiet after sacrifice.

The drawers, the Chinese drawers:
even pulling them out
from the bodies of the *five evil breeds*—
a Red Book must be in there.

(Translated by Arthur Sze)

输掉了

输掉了是一个美妙的词
我们把贫困输掉了
我们把痛苦输掉了
我们把疾病输掉了
问题是输给谁
哪一家赌场
哪一届政府
甚至
哪一位上帝有如此的雅量
接下来的问题是
我们的雅量更大
我们一直在赢

Lost

is a wonderful word
I put a bet on poverty and I lost
I put a bet on pain and lost
I bet on sickness and lost
the problem is who I lost to—
which gambling house
which government
even which god
can take all that on board
the next problem is
my tolerance seems even greater—
I keep winning

(Translated by W.N. Herbert)

杨炼

个人地理学

别人看不见
比高地更高 有乌鸦白茫茫的领空
公园抖动它的绿 抖着
子宫壁上的肌肉 分娩
花瓣哭成一片的春天
手掌上满载故事的地图
斜斜织入这条街 什么也不说
就变了 树木的密码锁
一拨一个去年 再拨
压死的鸟鸣都跃回枝头
水耽于幻想 万物的孤独
嵌在一枚人形的图钉上
别人看不见 阳光锤打中
你无知地跨进这个下午
跟着黑暗的指南

Yang Lian

Personal Geography

                    Others can not see
the blank airspace of crows higher than the hill
the park convulsing its green   convulsing
the womb-wall muscle   giving birth
to spring cried out by the petals in their expanse
    The map of your palm holds all of the stories
weaves slantwise into this street   says nothing
but has changed   the combination lock of the trees
spins back one past year   and spins again
and all the birdsong crushed to death flips back into the branches
water indulges its own fantasies   the loneliness of all things
nailed by a hook in human form
    Others can not see   under the hammering sun
you walk unknowing into this afternoon
following a guidebook of darkness

(Translated by Antony Dunn)

鬼魂奏鸣曲

一、 海与河

跨出栅栏就是大海
而两条鱼的克星 还要
一刹那更多的黑暗

跨出栅栏了 波浪的摇椅
摇着悬崖的突兀
每过一夜就再升高一点

他们的肉体
与脚下一阵阵涛声押韵
溢满他们的盲目

每个小小洞穴都湿淋淋的
每次呼吸都没有岸
他们彼此的楔形地带

彼此嵌入
咸腥的舔食在海面上漂流
礁石间一点灯火在哪个世纪

一亮 大海漏进手心
记忆有河水的本地口音
悬崖夜夜升高 崩塌已追上鸟翅了

栅栏之外 他们
偶然停在哪儿 就留在那儿
任一股黑潮从内心涌出

二、 乐曲－花园

他们能看见那针管
推着致命的液体
这床边的黑

Ghost Sonatas

1. Ocean and River

Beyond the fence there's only ocean
but the cursed fish-star still sucks
more darkness from this moment.

Beyond the fence, surging waves
shake the sheer cliff.
Every night they rear higher.

Our bodies rhyme
with the pounding surf beneath our feet—
a blinding flood.

Every little hole is drenched.
Every breath is shoreless.
Our bodies' coastlines

wedge into each other.
We lick salt from the sea's skin.
In what century was that lamp among the rocks

lit? The sea swishes in our palms.
Memory has a river's tongue.
The cliff rises higher each night to collapse at the wings of birds.

Beyond the fence where we happened
to stop, we will always pause
to loose a black tide from our hearts.

2. The Music-Garden

Night's syringe
shoots a lethal dose
of darkness around our bed.

被乐曲浮雕着
花园的轮廓在返回
会呻吟的蕊　鲜艳就是返回

耻骨湿润　旋转
音符一尾一尾游离磁带
注射到深处　烛光摇着无限远

鬼魂暴露在隘口上
鬼魂的演奏　只挑选
肉质的隘口

那自幽香中反复成形的
蹂躏一枚花瓣　四季满室萦绕
他们带着上路的每一夜

都和星座一样大
按下黑暗的循环键　再唱
但什么也不能延迟

但鬼魂灌溉的
鬼魂还热烈采摘着　挣脱
鳞　即兴的死又刷新即兴的生

Carved by music,
the garden's contours are returning.
A gasping corolla bursts into colour.

Our wet crotches
wrench musical notes from the cassette. One after the other they float up—
injected to the hilt. A candle flickers in deep space.

A ghost appears in the narrow pass.
It has chosen only the narrow pass of flesh
for its performance,

an endlessly recurring fragrance,
petal-trampling—all the seasons conjured in our room.
Every night the ghost ushers in

is huge as a constellation.
We press the rewind key for darkness to sing again
but nothing can be put off.

That which we water
the ghost passionately plucks, releasing us
from our scales. An improvised death renews our improvised life.

(Translated by Pascale Petit)

饕餮之问

北极星嵌在额头正中
幽蓝　晶亮　瞳如冰
毁了一切 被烹煮的少女
孤零零怀抱着一切?

逃出安阳　逃进殷之夜
没别的光除了这目光
奢华磨洗一把大钺
粉嫩的残肢吻落在哪儿?

千百年　抬头
我们就在陷落　水切齿
总在下面　少女坍塌为哗哗声
攫　或者嚼?

千百个字再分裂还是
唯一那个　一笔写尽流淌的
烹煮一万次　肉仍浸着忧伤
醒来　攫　恰是嚼?

这张脸比不在更无情地
存在　这种无力
盯着谁就把谁凿穿成隘口
磨啊　什么美不是血淋淋的?

浅浅的青铜上浮雕着
我们浅浅的漂浮　瞳之轴
冷冷一问又把天空变小?
命名之黑里多少不升不降的太阳?

少女婀娜自殷之夜
荡回　一缕香捻熄了灯火吗?
人面兽面都温驯依偎进了轻烟吗?
什么也不说的语言　已完成了祭祀吗?

Questions about the Demon Taotie

The Pole Star is set in the centre of his forehead.
The deep blue   is crystalline   his icy pupil
has destroyed everything   Does the lonely
boiled girl embrace everything?

Escaping from Anyang   is an escape into the Yin night
No other light except this sight
luxuriously grinding a huge axe
Where did the tender broken limbs fall?

Looking up   for thousands of years
we sink down   Water always grinds its teeth
beneath us   the girl collapsing to a gurgle
Does Taotie seize   or chew?

Thousands of words re-split open are still
the one character   that one stroke captures life's flow
has been cooked ten thousand times   the flesh still soaked in sorrow
to reawaken   Is seizing   chewing?

This face is even more ruthless
than non-being   this powerlessness
staring out rams a hole
to pound away   What beauty is not bloody?

Our floating life is carved
on the shallow bronze relief   Does
the eye's axle icily shrink space?
How many suns don't rise or set in the darkness of naming?

The girl swings gracefully back from the Yin
night   Does a thin fragrance snuff out all light?
Do bestial and human faces gently clasp vapour?
Has unutterable language   finally fulfilled the sacrifice?

(Translated by Pascale Petit)

一粒葵花籽的否定句
——致A.W.W.

不能想象这瓷制的江水中
曾泊着杜甫的扁舟
我不认识月光　只看见诗句的皎洁
在一行行衰减　至无人
至象征　谈论一切又回避一切
我不是象征　死在一粒葵花籽硬壳下的太阳
也不是　孩子们雪白坍塌的肉
并没有消失　一条破晓的地平线不可能
忘了那阵疼　骨头被玻璃切开时像玻璃
来不及叫喊才不得不在每天的曙光中叫喊
一场地震不会停止
一种窒息不在死后　种植到天边的栅栏
铐着更难堪的沉默　因此　我不怕
年轻女警察审视我的裸体
它被烧制成形　和你的并无区别
不知道别的碎除了亿万次加深自己的碎
不落进泥土　只落进流不动的江水中
不在乎石头含着的金黄　得继续
含着　像滴杜甫的老泪
不让这首诗沉沦为冷漠死寂的美

A Sunflower Seed's Lines of Negation
(For Ai Weiwei)

      unimaginable that Du Fu's little boat was once
           moored on this ceramic river
    I don't know the moonlight   see only the poem's clarity
        attenuated line by line   to a non-person
   to the symbols   discussing and avoiding everything
I'm no symbol   a sun dying under the sunflower seed's hard shell
    nor is the sun   snow-white collapsed meat of children
   nor have I disappeared   daybreak's horizon impossibly
      forgot that pain   bones like glass sliced by glass
      I didn›t scream, so must scream at each first light
         an earthquake never stands still
no need to suffocate the dead   planting rows of fences to the ends
              of the earth
   handcuffing ever more shameful silence   so   I don't fear
   the young policewoman interrogating my naked body
      it was formed by fire   no different to yours
knowing no other way to shatter but a hundred million shatterings
             within myself
    falling into no soil   only into the river that can't flow
that cares nothing for the yellow flower within the stone   having to
              go on
     to hold back   like a drop of Du Fu's old tears
 refusing to let the poem sink into dead indifferent beauty

(Translated by Brian Holton and W.N. Herbert)

散步者

水下的金鱼是否会歌唱一座城市的兴衰
河边一排钻研羽毛的天鹅
是否在刻划　揽镜自照的少女
风声灌满了他散步的自我
　　　　被黑暗中一条街领着
到这片沼泽里　脚陷下一寸深
绿漫出堤岸熟读冬天的无奈
一场雨后　草叶破碎的膝盖到处跪着
一块云虚构一次日蚀
他在地平线远眺中忽明忽暗
　　　　繁衍有只雁整整叫过的一夜
到这个遗忘里
感觉被河谷温柔地吞下去
感觉自己已变成河谷　一株枯柳
爆炸的金色　投掷一只不停分娩天空的子宫
　　　　听木栅栏在风中呼啸
　　　　被钉死才拦住日子
到达水和血湿漉漉的相似性
沉溺等在这儿　小酒馆絮絮叨叨的未来
锁着门　一城市的他端着冷了的杯子
　　　　像个被栽种的呼吸
走得更远　埋进老铁桥的骸骨
不可能再远　大丛暗红锈蚀的灌木
逼入窗户　阳光鬼魅地一亮
提示他头上定居的阴沉沉的水位
　　　　呛死的风景到了
　　　　黑暗中拆散的
　　　　　　　孤悬的台阶到了

Stroller

Whether the golden fish sing about the rise and fall of the city or not
a line of swans on the riverbank study the book of their feathers
whether they model girls with mirrors or not
the stroller's self is filled completely by the sound of the wind
        led by a pitch-dark street
towards this stretch of marshland   where feet sink in an inch
the banks overflow with green which knows winter's weakness only too well
after the rain   the grassblades kneel on broken knees
one cloud invents an eclipse
the horizon watches him abruptly change between light and dark
        breeding a night
        in which a wild goose calls him continuously
towards this act of forgetting
feeling softly swallowed by the valley
feeling he has already become the valley   an empty willow
whose golden explosion throws out a womb endlessly giving birth to the sky
        listening to the wooden fence shout in the wind
        so nailed to death it stops the days
he arrives at the shared wetness of water and blood
where drowning waits   the chattering future a little bar
with a locked door   he is the entire city holding a stone cold cup
        as though planted, panting
walking further to be buried in the skeleton of an old iron bridge
walking impossibly further   rusty blood-red bushes
burst through his window   ghost-like sunlight appears once
revealing the swollen dark water-level settled over his head
        the drowned landscape is here
        in the dark the separated
                lonely hanging step is here

(Translated by W.N. Herbert)

紫郁金宫：慢板的一夜

后宫里的一夜总有月光　玉阶和珠帘
却都是想象的　一束花衬着壁纸的蓝
想象　妃子的紫衣下一堆雪在坍塌
急急等待被占用的雪　用结晶慢慢
转身　每分钟向内卷曲着慢慢舞蹈
一束郁金香璀璨的衰败脱下一场自恋
一种紫色的耳语　必须喘息着说
只对那人说　当他重重碾压着花瓣
一滴紫色的奶　像妃子急急等待被吸尽的
想着　全世界就涌进一根滚烫的脉管

后宫里的火　总有舌头百般的顽皮
被修剪的尖　舔到皮肤的空　午夜之绿
绿如片片堆叠在妃子脚踝处的叶子
那人的宠爱　一场来自所有方向的沐浴
浇淋他的花　乳头的紫玉小碗斟满了
报复一个时间　大海沉积在色素里
一束郁金香一夜从女高音滑入女中音
今夜　霸道之美对称着流逝的诗意
妃子只为那人保存的幽香　只交给他把玩
紫色的慢慢粉碎　丝光停不住时

后宫里总有闪烁成一个蕊的磷光
一根针指挥着　肉体四季被演奏的欲望
一种镂空的剪裁　镂空至妃子的生死
壁纸蓝蓝如一次缝合所有伤痛的狂想
只一次　花影中日子咬下的牙印
无限发暗　这夜色无限鲜嫩　刺绣到身上
原初那次　紫　像滴慢慢洇开的奶
慢慢被宇宙吸收　纵容那人的黄　那么黄
凝视中赐给妃子一个黑尽的语法
当花瓶像个词圆圆贴着手掌

A Night in the Purple Tulip Palace (Adagio)

In this seraglio night always consists of   moonlight, jade steps and a
                                                       curtain of pearls
all imaginary   a bunch of flowers against blue wallpaper
imagine   caving in under the concubine's clothes a mound of snow
snow waiting impatiently to be possessed   its crystalline body slowly
turning   constantly curling in on itself in a slow dance
a bunch of tulips divesting itself of the love of self as it brightly declines
a kind of purple whisper   which must be spoken breathily
addressing only him   as he crushes the petals heavily
a drop of purple milk   like a concubine impatiently waiting to be sucked
concentrating   the entire world into one burning duct

In this seraglio   fire always has the rude playfulness of tongues
a pointed tip   licks the emptiness of skin   midnight's cling
green like leaves gathered at the concubine's ankles
his preference for her   a shower coming from every angle
watering the flower   the little purple bowl of her nipple fills
in revenge against time   the pigment holds ocean's deepest spoils
a bunch of tulips slips in a single night from soprano to mezzo
tonight   tyrannous beauty is balanced by this aesthetic of erosion
this evasive scent which the concubine keeps for him alone   and only
                                                       lets him savour
when the silky light can't stop   purple very gently splays open

In this seraglio there's always this dead bone phosphor light becoming
                                                       a pistil's gleam
conducting the body's desire   to be played for all four seasons
carving out this hole cut through   the concubine's sculpted days
the wallpaper is blue like a crazy mind sewing up all past pains
only once   the hours' bitemarks into each flower
darken endlessly   the night is stitched onto flesh   endlessly fresh
                                                       and tender
once in the beginning   purple   gradually spread like a drop of milk
slowly absorbed by the universe   which sees his lasciviousness   and winks
by staring he bestows on the concubine a totally dark grammar
the vase is like a word resting between the hands

(Translated by W.N. Herbert)

蝴蝶——纳博科夫

这些最小　　最绚丽的洛丽塔
嘴里含着针一样的叫声
大气显微镜　　远眺深藏起闪光的虎牙

　　　　　　你胖了　　口音还慢得像雪花
　　　　　　擎着路灯那张古怪的采集网
　　　　　　赴一个标本册的幽会

显微的激情扑向总被搓碎的
翅膀的草图　　留在搬空的房间里
每个诗人身边翩翩流浪的塔玛拉*

　　　　　　像白日梦舅舅掸下的粉末
　　　　　　一只蝴蝶有时比劫难更难懂
　　　　　　你　　幸福的大叫和风格不是无辜的

翻动　　锁在空中的射杀父亲的子弹
孵化成彩色课本　　一场雪仍在下
死者们绕着青春的蕊

　　　　　　而照片上的眼睛盯视最长的一刹那
　　　　　　飞到天尽头一定不够
　　　　　　得学书页　　蜕掉一张人皮

才认出一枚卵精致的大爆炸
往昔是朵搂紧你的雏菊
塔玛拉　　总带着树丛　　微黑　　轻弹双翼

　　　　　　你珍爱的变形优雅叠加
　　　　　　叼起世界　　用一根针钉住的高
　　　　　　虎啸　　全不理睬记忆的聋哑

---

*塔玛拉：纳博科夫自传《说吧，记忆》中，给真实的初恋情人杜撰出的名字。她和纳博科夫初识于一九一七年革命前，并在俄国南方流亡初期再次相遇

Butterfly – Nabokov

These smallest   most iridescent Lolitas
Held a needling scream inside their mouths
The air a microscope looking over   the deep hidden glimmering tiger's
                                                            teeth

    You're getting fatter   accent still slow as snowflower
    Holding high   the weird collecting net, the streetlamp
    To make the tryst   in a specimen volume

A microscopic passion is always pouncing on sketches of wings
Always twisted & broken   left behind in an emptied room
Next to every poet is a Tamara, dancing   flying

    Like powder brushed off a daydream Uncle
    A butterfly is sometimes more difficult to understand than a catastrophe
    Your   blissful shouting & high style is not so innocent

Turn the page   the bullet heading straight for the father is locked in the air
And hatching   to become the colorful textbook   the same snow still
                                                                         falling
The dead in orbiting flutter   around the pistil of youth

    And the eyes in the photos staring on the longest moment
    It's sure not enough to fly to the age of sky
    You must learn to be the pages of a book   to moult the human skin

Then to recognize the exquisite cosmic explosion from a single egg
The past, a daisy that hugs you tightly
Tamara   always carries trees lightly darker   tremulously beating wings

    The transmutation you cherish   elegantly laid down in layers
    Holding up the world in its mouth   nailed on high by a needle
    A tiger roars   indifferent to deaf-mute memory

(Translated by Joshua Weiner)

蝴蝶——柏林

父亲的墓地　被更多墓地深深
盖住　塌下来的石头像云
夯实的重量里一只薄翼意外析出

　　　　　一跳一跳找到你　当你还英俊
　　　　　细长　着迷于花朵摇荡的小扇子
　　　　　公园中器官烫伤器官的吻

空气的阻力也得学
墙　死死按住彩绘的肩膀
暮色垂落　反衬小小明艳的一跃

　　　　　当你的心惊觉这一瞬
　　　　　一座城市已攥紧你绝命的籍贯
　　　　　老　没有词　只有扼在咽喉下的呻吟

才懂得反叛越纤弱　越极端
一种长出金黄斑点的力
推开水泥波浪　只比世界高一寸

　　　　　海蝴蝶　不奢望迁徙出恐怖
　　　　　飞啊　塔玛拉和父亲　粼粼
　　　　　扛着身体　轻拍下一代流亡者入眠

灰烬的目录没有最远处
你栖在醒来　就脱掉重量的住址上
树叶暗绿的灯罩挪近

　　　　　当你　不怕被一缕香撅住
　　　　　成为那缕香　遗物般递回一封信
　　　　　打着海浪的邮戳：柏林

Butterfly – Berlin

The father's grief   sinks deeply into many more griefs
Covered   stone crushing like cloud
A great weight tamping down   and surprisingly out from under it a
                                                thin wing

    Leaping to find you   when you were still comely
    Slender   captivated by the swaying flower fanning itself
    In the park   one organ burning another, a kiss

The obstruction of the air must be learned
The wall   tightly pressing the colorful painted shoulder
The falling evening color   sets off a little shining leap

    When your heart suddenly feels this moment
    This city holds tightly your ancestral origin, your fated ending
    Old age has no words   but only the choked back moan

Then to know   the thinner betrayal is the more extreme
One kind of force driving the golden yellow eyespot to grow
Pushing open the concrete waves   floating above the world only by an inch

    The sea butterfly   doesn't dream of migrating far from Terror
    Flying   Tamara and the father   flickering
    Carrying bodies   lightly pat to sleep the next generation of exiles

The ashes' contents have no horizon
You perch at the address   where upon waking you shrug off the weight
                                                of home
The leaves' dark green lampshade moves closer

    When you don't fear   to be caught by a thread of fragrance
    You yourself are becoming the fragrance   delivering back the letter the
dead left
    Bearing its stamp of ocean waves: Berlin

(Translated by Joshua Weiner)

杨小滨

目的论

为眉毛而拔剑相向
为嘴唇而叶落
为诗而爱情
为理想而屠杀

为蝴蝶而染上疾病
为风暴而革命
为沙漠,为心中的骆驼
血管早已枯干

为星辰而布满钉子
为阳光而失明
为了明天,死亡的今天就已注定
而明天不过是另一次今天

Yang Xiaobin

Teleology

Confronting each other with swords in the name of eyebrows
Leaves falling in the name of lips
Romance in the name of poetry
Genocide in the name of the ideal

Contracting a disease in the name of butterflies
Starting a revolution in the name of a tempest
In the name of the desert, of the camel deep in the heart,
blood vessels shrivelling up

Scattering iron nails in the name of stars
Going blind in the name of sunlight
Dooming the death of today in the name of tomorrow,
rendering tomorrow only another today

(Translated by John Gery)

裸露

她走进旧照片洗澡,把水搅混
象表层的泛黄。我
用雾气擦亮镜框,但看不清
是谁,藏在浴帘背后。

"一个少女,"她解释说,
"但不是我。"她扔出
更多的鳞片、污垢、内衣
婚礼上的歌谱。"是美人鱼吗?"
我问得她大笑,水珠
溅在我脸上。"让我念一段
诗经,"她声音宛转而空洞

我听不懂。我捂住耳朵
我飞逃,撞在她身上
才从梦里醒来:"原来
你在这儿。"她漂在玻璃上
默许:"因为
你在梦中跑得太快。"

她擦干,一边哼歌
一边打喷嚏。远远地
她下颌的倒影
悬挂在春天的颈项。
"那是一件礼品,"她喃喃而语,
"我遗忘已久。"

她脱去无数冬天的积雪。
我给她点烟。照片在火苗里
弯曲。"对不起,"我说,
而她消逝无踪。

Nude

She entered an old photograph to bathe,
stirring the water, a murky yellow glaze. I
rubbed the foggy glass but couldn't make out
the figure concealed behind the curtain.

"A young woman," she offered,
"but not me." She tossed out
bloodstained scales, specks of dirt, lingerie,
the songbook for a wedding. "Are you a mermaid?"
She laughed at my question, splashing water
onto my face. "Let me recite for you,"
she purred, but in her disembodied voice, her words

faded into nothing. I covered my ears
and fled, until I crashed into her body,
jolting me awake: "Ah ha,
so there you are." Floating on the glass,
she smiled compliantly. "You were
running too fast in your dream."

Humming to herself, she dried herself off,
then sneezed. In the distance
the reflection of her chin
glimmered around the neck of spring.
"Here is my gift for you," she murmured,
"something I long ago overlooked,"

as she stripped thick layers of snow from her body.
I lit her a cigarette. The photograph,
catching fire, began to warp. "Forgive me," I sighed,
as she vanished in a wisp of smoke.

(Translated by John Gery)

景色与情节

她湿漉漉地跑过来，身后的影子
象彗星，雪白，她说
"我们去看电影。"我
听见更多的呼吸声，在夜里
"我们去吃冰激凌。"她说

但我没有时间。我转身
她又站在我身边，从胸前
掏出半只苹果，手上血红
好像苹果是头颅。但
我要赶去梦里。我急急
穿好睡衣，坐到藤椅上。
她拨动纽扣："我要回到晴天。"

那真是一个鲜艳的周末。我们赶路
没有看见碾在路旁的松鼠
只看见湖，易碎的湖面
我不忍心跳进去。她的手颤抖着
好像濒死的鱼。她的眼睛
充溢着泪水，最后滴在丁当的船舷。
"太甜了，"她舔着阳光
舌尖一闪一闪，象灯塔
从黑洞洞的嘴里。

但我没有时间。我回头
是另一个她，"我们去挖牡蛎。"
我听见雷声。她说
"快，快，"一边脱下外衣
风刮着两颊，枝叶间的笑声
越来越冷，她挎着篮子
手和双乳陷在泥沙里。
"午睡，然后才是晚餐。"
我的目光朝着水面移动。
但她并未察觉："就一会儿。"

我脸上爬满了蚂蚁，象交响乐里
一支柔板的咬啮。

The Setting and the Plot

Drenched, she rushed up to me, the shadow behind her
as white as a comet, and proclaimed,
"Let's go to the movies!" I,
because it was night, could only hear her panting.
"Let's go out for ice cream!" she begged me

but I had no time. I turned away
and there she was, beside me again, plucking an apple
from her chest, her hands bloody
as though she'd pulled out a baby's head. Still,
I was sucked deeper into the dream. Quickly
I slipped into my pyjamas and settled into the wicker chair.
Tugging at my buttons, she cried, "I want to go back into tomorrow."

It turned out to be a colorful weekend. We pushed on with our journey
not spying a single squirrel in the ditch beside us
but only the lake, with its shimmering surface
I didn't have the heart to leap into. Her hands twitched
like two dying fish. Her opaque eyes,
welling over with tears, suddenly caused our boat to rock.
Licking the sunlight, she exclaimed, "It tastes too sweet,"
as her tongue glistened, beaming like a beacon
from the dark hole of her mouth.

But I had no time. I turned my back
only to find another her: "Let's go digging for oysters!"
I heard a thunderclap. She shouted,
"Hurry! Hurry!" as she tore off her coat.
The wind battered her cheeks, and a cackle in the bushes
grew colder and colder. She grabbed a bucket
and burrowed with her hands, her breasts brushing the sand.
"First, a nap, then dinner."
My eyes looked toward the water.
But she didn't notice: "Just for a little while."

Soon ants began to crawl across my cheeks
in a symphonic adagio.

我是否把脸遗忘在原地?
但谁也没有找到。在梦里
我只听见她又说
"把窗帘打开。"但我害怕
阳光般的鸟。我披上窗帘
躺在过去的船上,等待梦中之梦。

她说,"最后一次吧。"
好像几年前的声音。我抬头
她从门后一闪而过。我再次
闭上眼睛,阳光涌进整个房间。
"是咖啡还是焦味?"她尖叫。

离题的情歌

1
我睁开你的眼睛。我无法凝视的
眼睛,让我失明。
让我瞥见的花朵
在你的春意中阑珊,你一回眸
我的美人就苍老无比。
你一转眼,风景把我席卷而去。
我看见的,就是你
眼底的海,是你的目光
淹没了我。是我清晨醒来的时分
一只瞳人般的鸟飞去
带走了你,和你镜中的睡姿。

2
我张开你的嘴唇。我无法亲吻的
嘴唇,你饮的酒
灌醉了我。我歌唱
你的声音刺痛我。我忍受
你的饥渴,我吞食
你嘴里的花园纷纷飘落

Did I abandon my face there?
But no one has found it. In the dream
I could hear her voice once again:
"Raise the curtain." But I feared
the birdlike sunlight. I held the curtain draped over my shoulders
reclining in what had once been the boat, waiting for the dream inside
      my dream.

She whispered, "How about one more time?"
in a voice familiar from years before. I lifted my head
only to glimpse her flashing by the door. Finally,
I closed my eyes. Sunlight gushed into the room.
"Do you smell coffee or is something burning?" she cried.

(Translated by John Gery)

Love Song Gone Awry

1
I am blinking with your eyes, the eyes
I cannot gaze at, that blind me.
Whatever flowers I glimpse
wither in spring. When you look behind,
my beautiful woman there grows wrinkled.
When you look to the side, the landscape sweeps me away.
If I peer into the ocean at the bottom of your eyes,
your vision
drowns me. When I awake at dawn
a bird flies from your eyes, taking in its beak
the image in the mirror of you sleeping.

2
I am pouting with your lips, the lips
I cannot kiss. The wine you drink
befuddles me. When I start singing,
your voice pierces me. I suffer
your thirst. I swallow
the gardens inside your mouth drifting

我吐出你的早餐
你的絮语,你的尖叫。
静下来,让我用你的舌头
说话,那一句
你的梦呓,我遗忘已久。

3
我伸出你的手。我无法握住的手
穿过黑夜,拥抱我的阴影。
我捏成你的拳头
你用手背上的月色
掀倒了我。是我握住的指甲
刻出你的掌纹,是我
用窗外的风抚摸你的伤口
我疼痛。我的手指战栗
插入你的呼救,用你
在我内心的双手
剪断我的祷词,扼住我的呼吸。

信件·面包·书签(三首)

信件

午餐之前,你听见信封里的叫喊。
你把它打开:一封
寄自本埠的情书,落款是
小夜曲。

你坚持把它封死。就象
埋掉一只夜莺。你怕

那首歌。你把它扔回邮筒
直到第二天
它又在你的信箱里呻吟

downward from the sky
and exhale your breakfast, your whisper, your scream.
Quiet now: Let me speak with your tongue
the words you whisper in your sleep, the words I
have never heard.

3
I am extending your hand, the hand
I fail to touch, seizing my shadow, piercing the night.
When my hand closes into your fist, you
push me away
into moonlight. These are my fingernails
that carve your palm print, fondling
your bruises in the night breeze,
causing me pain. My fingers tremble,
breaking through your cry, as your
hands reach inside my chest,
cut short my pleading, and begin to strangle me.

(Translated by John Gery)

Three Short Poems

1. The Letter

Before lunch, you heard a cry come from inside the envelope.
You opened it: a
love letter from across town, signed
"Serenade."

You carefully resealed it, as though
burying a nightingale. Such pure music

terrifies you. You dropped it off at the post office
but the next day
you heard it in your mailbox again, weeping.

面包

你用梳子切开面包。那里
有死者的发丝,娇嗔
烤热的爱。

面包越来越黑,碎屑
越来越理不清:

梳洗之前,你的脸已烧焦。
难以下咽的五官
带着美的饥饿。

书签

你打开一本尘封已久的书:
一只手
夹在书签的位置。

它不愿意离开,它死死地
抓住这个字
一个句号。

枯萎的手,书页上的化石
等待另一只手的掌声

2. Bread

You sliced the loaf of bread with a comb,
finding inside it hairs of the dead, a squeamish voice,
and dry, warmed-over love.

The bread turned darker and darker, its crumbs
more and more seared and shriveled:

Before you could wash and dress, your face too was burnt:
your senses' appetite for beauty
had become too hard to swallow.

3. The Bookmark

You opened a long neglected book:
A hand
was inserted in place of a bookmark.

Unwilling to let go, it held on tightly,
grasping at characters,
clinging to a period.

That poor shrunken hand, a relic on the page,
still waiting for another hand to clap with.

(Translated by John Gery)

于坚

在西部荒野中看见火车

那时我们站在旷野中间 以色列在西 莫高窟在北

仿佛从水里出来 火车再次开出大漠或者开回

摩西在车头上唱着歌 电线杆望尘莫及

车厢蠕动着 黑色的链条在滑出大地的轮子

不知道它运走了什么 不知道它运来过什么

我们站在旷野中间 捡起石块又扔掉

等着它走完剩下的铁轨 就像从未被运走的远古之人

Yu Jian

Watching a Train in the Western Wilderness

At that time we stood in the middle of the wilderness
        Israel persisted to the West
                the Mogao Caves to the North
As if coming forth from between the waters
        for a second time
                the steam train appeared from the Gobi
                    or disappeared into it
Moses was on the footplate singing psalms
        wooden pylons watched the dust
              but couldn't catch it
The carriages shivered and snaked
        black pistons drove the wheels round
Not knowing what was being carried away
        what was being carried back
we stood in the middle of the wilderness
        picking up stones
               then casting them aside
waiting for the train to pass over the remaining rails
        as if the earliest people had never been carried away

(Translated by W.N. Herbert)

臧棣

自我表现协会

我喜欢诗中的散文——
它就像一群蝴蝶吸在大象的身上,
大象刚刚走出灌木。

移动的大象表情放松,
如同一队正在非洲度假的哑剧演员。
它们脚下的湿地像一张老照片。

而头脑僵硬的家伙们总也不能适应
大象背上的蝴蝶。
他们叫嚷,蝴蝶应该呆在泉水旁。

我喜欢诗中的散文胜于
诗中的诗。相信我,因为我
既不是大象,也不是蝴蝶。

2005.1.

Zang Di

The Self-Expression Association

In poetry I enjoy prose—
prose is like a swarm of butterflies clinging to an elephant's body.
The elephant has just emerged from the bushes.

The elephant has the relaxation of
a mime troupe on vacation in Africa.
The wetland beneath their feet looks like an old photo.

However some narrow-minded people find it difficult to accept
the butterflies on the elephant's back.
They protest that butterflies belong above a small pond.

I enjoy prose in poetry more than
a poem in poetry. Because, believe me, I
am neither the elephant nor the butterfly.

(Translated by Murray Edmond)

生活是怎么炼成的丛书

节目单上,风景已排到了
不起眼的地方。难怪。最近的账单
越来越像节目单。房租要交,
房贷要还,每样吃的东西都已被污染,
那么小的胃,矛盾于我们很渺小,
竟然一直在替宇宙冒险。
人心紧挨着绞肉机。每个机会
都像是深渊之间的缝隙。
比钢铁是怎样炼成的,还要极端的是,
生活是怎样炼成的。魔鬼训练
人人都有份,用不着担心你会不过了关。
凡想催眠现实的人,最终都难免
被现实催眠。凡是用运气解决的事
最终都变成了一种暧昧的耻辱。
死亡不再是一种平静,而是一种愤怒,
一种深奥的冷漠,有点像
死亡是怎么炼成的。每个人
都死过不止一次。活着,像是植物栽培,
并且被分散在不同的地方——
你的根,在这里,你的叶子,在那边,
你的花,在你不知道的地方插在
你从未见过的瓶子里。有趣的工作
还是看你爱不爱动手,它就像是
给希望换轮胎。假如超速了,
绝望不会被罚款。假如诗不能救你,
其他的启示肯定更微妙。
死亡不再像以往能中断任何事情,
但旅行却可以。大河在奔涌,
旅行就像从激流的河水中抽回
一只脚。票一点都不紧张,
你在这里买不到电影票,在那里
肯定能买到车票。记住,
车票不止是车票,同时还是电影票。
难怪。车票还可能同时是彩票。
人的风景正将人从风景中
推向只出售单程票的那个窗口。

How Life is Smelted

In the playbill, the scenery has been trundled off to
some unobtrusive place. It's no wonder. Recently, restaurant bills
have increasingly resembled playbills. Rent must be paid,
home loans must be repaid, all the different edibles have been polluted,
such tiny stomachs, their conflict with us is insignificant
save that they have always stood in for the risks of the cosmos.
The people's heart brushes against the meat grinder. Each opportunity
seems like a crack in the abyss.
What is more extreme than the method of smelting steel
is the smelting of life. In the training that is Hell Week
everyone's got their part, no use worrying that you won't pass through.
People who want to hypnotize reality, in the end they can't avoid
being hypnotized by reality. All problems resolved through good fortune,
in the end they become a kind of vague humiliation.
Death is no longer a form of serenity, it is a wrath,
a profoundly cold detachment, it's a little bit like
the way death itself is smelted. Each of us
has died many times. Living is like a plant growing,
and plus it has been scattered across many locations—
your roots here, your leaves over there,
your flowers in some unknown location, stuck in some bottle
you've never seen before. Interesting work
still depends on whether you like to set to or not, it's like
changing the tires on hope. If you decide to speed,
desperation won't be fined. If poetry cannot save you,
other enlightenments are surely more subtle.
Death can't interrupt affairs like it used to,
but travel can. The great river rushes and bubbles,
travelling is like pulling back one foot
from the torrential river current. No need to worry about tickets:
they don't sell movie tickets here, but over there
you can definitely get a bus ticket. Remember
that bus tickets are not just bus tickets, they are also movie tickets.
It's no wonder. Bus tickets can also be lottery tickets.
The human landscape is pushing humanity out of the landscape
towards the kiosk where they sell the one-way ticket.

(Translated by Nicholas Admussen)

牵线人丛书

看什么，都必须要先转过脸去，
这就是她。假如是直接面对，
她会比地震中的一条狗还要紧张。
怎么看世界，都不如一只猫那样顺眼。

她有时会控制不住在人狗之间有一种比较。
她对待猫比对待狗更严肃。
她曾说服自己要像爱猫一样爱上一个人。
她的结论是，爱怎么比数学还难。

她苦于灵魂不愿被束缚，
与她为敌的事物里，有大学，地铁和电视。
电视里的野兽会从屏幕里跑出来，舔她的眉毛和耳环。
这样的事，好像不止发生过好几回。

于是，每一样需要接触的东西
最终都变成了一种需要克服的事情。
她对环境有特殊的敏感。她不断地换环境——
在一个地方待太久了，人就会变成废墟。

于是，她比任何人都更频繁地从废墟中走出来。
这似乎是她不可抗拒的规律。
她自己偶尔也能认识到这一点。
新欢中已有无人能意识到的瑕疵，

她受不了瑕疵。或者说，她受不了
别人也会有她身上的那些瑕疵。
不完全是需要缓和矛盾的问题，
记忆里，旧爱在缥缈中似乎稍好一点。

洗脑算什么。腰被洗了，
才是被洗彻底了。她知道这个世界上
存在着用腰思考的人。下面垫得再高点，
她也许会在最遥远的地方看见这首诗的尾巴。

A Puppeteer

When looking at something, you must first turn your head
and that's her. If the gaze is direct
she will be jumpier than a dog in an earthquake.
There's no way to look at the world that's prettier than a single cat.

Sometimes she cannot suppress comparisons between people and dogs.
She treats cats in a much more serious way than she does dogs.
Once she convinced herself that she would love a person as much as cats.
Her conclusion was that loving something is more difficult than all math.

She will not have the suffering of her soul restrained,
among the objects that are her enemies are the university, subways, and TV.
The wild beasts in the TV can spring from the screen, lick her eyebrows
        and earrings.
This type of thing seems to have happened repeatedly, unceasingly.

So everything with which she comes into contact
finally becomes something to be overcome.
She has special sensitivity to her surroundings. She changes them constantly—
if she stays in a place too long, people become ruins.

So, with more frequency than anyone else, she sets forth from the ruins.
This seems to be her irresistible rule of self-discipline.
Sometimes she herself can acknowledge this to be true.
In new love there is already the blemish that nobody sees yet,

and she can't stand a blemish. Or one could say that she can't stand
for anyone else to share the blemishes that are on her body.
It's not entirely a question of needing to soften the contradictions,
in memory, dimly viewed old loves seem a little bit nicer.

There's no point to brainwashing. When the crotch has been washed,
that means that the washing is thorough. She knows that in this world
there are those who think with their crotch. She'll aim a little higher
        next time,
and maybe from far afield, she'll be able to see the tail of this poem.

(Translated by Nicholas Admussen)

翟永明

菊花灯笼漂过来

菊花一点点漂过来
在黑夜 在周围的静
在河岸沉沉的童声里
菊花淡 淡出鸟影

儿童提着灯笼漂过来
他们浅浅的合唱里
没有恐惧 没有嬉戏 没有悲苦
只有菊花灯笼 菊花的淡
灯笼的红

小姐也提着灯笼漂过来
小姐和她的仆从
她们都挽着松松的髻
她们的华服盛装 不过是
丝绸 飘带和扣子
不过是走动时悉嗦乱响的
缨络 耳环 钗凤

小姐和小姐的乳娘
她们都是过来人
她们都从容地寻找
在夜半时面对月亮
小姐温柔 灯笼也温柔
她们漂呵漂
她们把平凡的夜
变成非凡的梦游

每天晚上
菊花灯笼漂过来
菊花灯笼的主人 浪迹天涯
他忽快忽慢的脚步
使人追不上
儿童们都跟着他成长

Zhai Yongming

The Chrysanthemum Lantern Is Floating Over Me

A chrysanthemum lantern is floating towards me.
In the enveloping silence of pitch darkness—
a low murmur of children on the riverbank.
The lantern is so sheer a bird's shadow shows through it.

The children's chorus floats over with the lantern.
There's no fear, no pain,
only the lantern, the lightness of chrysanthemums
and the red glow of its candle.

A young girl also floats over—
a girl and her maids,
their hair up,
their luxurious clothes nothing but
silk, ribbons and buttons,
nothing but tinkling tassels when they walk—
tassels, earrings, phoenix hairpins.

The young girl and her wet nurse
have known death.
They are both searching for something leisurely.
They face the midnight moon.
The girl is gentle and the light soft.
They float towards me
transforming the ordinary night
into a somnambulist trance.

Every night
the lantern floats over me.
Its owner wanders to the end of heaven,
his pace sometimes fast, sometimes slow.
No one can catch up with him,
the children grow up with him.

This is the story of the changing world and of the lantern.

这就是沧海和灯笼的故事
如果我坐在地板上
我会害怕那一股力量
我会害怕那些菊影 光影 人影
我也会忽快忽慢
在房间里丁当作响

如果我坐在沙发或床头
我就会欣赏
我也会感到自己慢慢透明
慢慢变色
我也会终夜含烟 然后
离地而起

第六月

夜里月黑风高 男孩子们练习杀人
粗野的麦田潜伏某种欲念
我闻到整个村庄的醉意

有半年光景我仰面看它
直到畸形的身躯变成无垠
它旋转 犹如门轴生了锈
人们酗酒作乐 无人注意我

但我从一堆又一堆垃圾中
听到它的回声来自地心
满身尘埃的人用手触摸
黑檀木桌的神秘裂纹
想起盛朝年间的传说
今晚将有月蚀 妻子在木盆里净身
眼中充满盲目的恐惧

天空抽搐着，对我讳莫如深
祖先土葬的坟地
从墙缝处 裂开无数失神的眼睛
翌晨，掘墓者发现
诸侯的床已被白蚁充满

If I sit on the floor
the chrysanthemum's shadow, the light's shadow and the shadows of people
frighten me
and I sometimes slowly, sometimes quickly
make a silvery sound in my room.

If I sit on the bed
I can enjoy this sensation
while I gradually turn transparent,
gradually change colour.
All night I merge into mist
then rise into the air.

(Translated by Pascale Petit)

Jing An Village, June

Moonless night—the wind is high and boys practise killing.
Desire stirs in the wild wheatfield—
I can smell the drunkenness of the village.

For half a year I stare at the moon
until this twisted body of mine melts
and the spinning moon is a rusted hinge.
Everybody is drinking, having fun—no-one
notices me. At the garbage heap
I can feel an echo from the very heart of the earth.

A dusty farmer touches a fissure
in the old ebony table.
I think of legends from the great dynasties.
Tonight there'll be a lunar eclipse
and the farmer's wife will take a bath,
her eyes full of blind fear.

The veiled sky shivers and shapeshifts.
In the graveyard where ancestors lie
the baked mud walls crack open with dead eyes.
At dawn, tomb diggers will find

我，我们偶然的形体
在黑暗中如何，在白昼也同样干枯

唐朝书生

唐朝书生 常常赶夜路
他们常常投宿于 陌生人家
赶考的日子很紧 书生们日夜兼程
他们常常磨光了脚底
也没能到达京城

沿路总有二三人家
沿路也总有一些小桥流水
祖母 母亲 和孙女
她们都有各自的不如意

书生们意兴萧索 或志气遄飞
端看他们怎样对待同等的事物：
——直取京城里遥远的金榜
还是面前那些女人们眼中的悲伤

the coffins crawling with termites.
My body—all the bodies we are born with
decay in the dark and the light.

(Translated by Pascale Petit)

Scholars of the Tang Dynasty

Scholars of the Tang Dynasty
Must frequently press on by night
But hope for lodging at a stranger's house.

Desperate to sit for the civil exams,
Although they walked their feet red raw
They were usually late, and besides

There were always distractions—
Small bridges with streams rushing under
Where grandmother, mother and daughter

Each offered her different sorrow.
The passing scholars, the ambitious
Would-be servants of the state, must choose:

To hasten on towards the distant capital
Where billboards would display the names of those
Who made the grade; or to marry the women

They met on the way, and thereafter
Be someone the locals could always
Regard as a failure, instead.

(Translated by Sean O'Brien)

张炜

松林

这是一片生长和站立的悲悯
你可以从它的肃穆和气息中
领悟那指向渺远的质询
如林的手臂久久伸向空阔
直到掌根生出了塔楼
直到塔楼装满了谶语
浓发压顶垂手而立
每一根松针落地都清晰可闻
这里的天籁浓缩成一个方方的硬块
小心地压上林中空地
此界与彼界的往事生出了胡须
创伤与苍老让大地不发一声
这里演练过多少残酷的嬉戏
这里践踏过多少棵草本植物

Zhang Wei

Pine Forest

On the coast of Longkou there is a vast forest of pine trees.

Here is a land of sorrow growing, of mercy standing still.
In its solemn breath you can feel the questioning of the far distance
                                          beyond seeing and knowing.
The arms of the forest reach forever into ampleness, into emptiness,
until the pagoda at the wrist grows and is full of prophesy.
The thick hair of the trees weighs on their heads,
                                          they stand with their hands low.
The fall of each needle can be heard clearly.
Here all the sounds of nature are cast into bright squares
laid carefully on the ground between the trees.
Here all the stories of the present and the past are bearded and stooped.
The earth is mute. Its bears its wounds and numberless age.
How many cruelties have been rehearsed and played out in this place.
How many grasses have been trampled and lost.

(Translated by Polly Clark)

周瓒

慢

知觉在恢复,从麻木日子的肘弯处
疼痛的慢,如爱的淡味
辣酱刺激胃口,夜宵能醒梦
喝红酒到微醉,血液也感受着
肉体的慢,或热的运行
坐着,坐着,坐在灯下
请求手指的舞步,领会
写作的慢,一生的
多少瞬间伴随着心灵的醒

未名湖

通向你的路被插上了标牌
探险的意义也就荡然无存
幸亏记忆被收藏得很紧
也许还一度被锁进了课桌
匆匆行走的脚步,比神色更叫人难忘
其中的一些,宁愿把围绕你的
环行称为锻炼,这恰好符合了
教育的暗示,水面也照鉴过
太多的脸孔,并不特别记下过哪一位
因此,说到一个故事
有人往往把它想象为一个事故

Zhou Zan

Slowness

The awareness, recovering from numb days like a blow to the elbow
the slowness of the pain   the plain scent of love
chilli sauce can pique the appetite   and a late supper stirs dreams
sip wine, get a little drunk   blood also feels
the slowness of the body   the spread of warmth
sitting, shifting, sitting under the desklamp
asking this dance of fingers to grasp
the slowness of the writing   how in life so many instants can be met by
the soul waking up

(Translated by W.N. Herbert)

Nameless Lake

Now the roads that lead to you are stuck with signs
so any sense of exploration has totally vanished.
Luckily, the memories have been hoarded up, perhaps they're locked in
    a desk.
Hurrying steps, unlike faces, can't be forgotten.
Some preferred to call the walk around you
"exercise"—this was just to keep in line with
the idea of education. Your surface once mirrored
too many faces, but didn't retain anyone special.
So when your tale is told, people think that's not an account, it's an
    accident.

(Translated by W.N. Herbert)

灰喜鹊

她总是听见它们的谈话
她破译着 像传说中的公冶长
它们中的一个从远方归来
兴致勃勃 讲述它的历险
其它的伙伴们争着嚷嚷 相信或
怀疑 拖长着音调 无比轻蔑呀
讲述者的声音不再欢快 好像
被揭穿了底似的 或者是累了 啊
是不屑于 不屑于同无知者罗嗦
而妈妈总是骂她 说话的担子
闭嘴吧 灰喜鹊
你个子小 也挑不动担子
而某一天 一只灰喜鹊
死在高大的槐树下 像是从
睡眠的窝巢中跌下
尖嘴闭得紧紧 而她
年龄太小 破译不了死的沉默

Jay

I always heard their talk,
could translate it like Gong Ye-chang
who understood the language of birds.
One of the jays returned from a far journey,
full of herself, chattering about her adventures.
The other jays screeched at her, some believed
some doubted. They made such a racket
that the taleteller raised her voice, long and loud,
proudly at first, then sad
to have told her secrets. She was so tired,
refused to enlighten these fools.
And mum always criticised me, called me a burden of talk.
"Shut up Jay
you're too small, you can't even carry things."
But one day a jay fell
from the nest of sleep
and died under the locust tree,
her beak firmly closed, too young
to translate death's silence.

(Translated by Pascale Petit)

英诗中译

English into Chinese

安敏轩

驾车旅行

  敞篷车现在是一列火车。可折叠的火车现在是一个秘密仪式里的摩门教徒,列车驶向神圣的使命。以美元计算的价格,现在用人民币计算,陷入盲目崇拜的人民币。在中国,由于人们更喜欢循环的空气,而将列车间的大多数车门紧闭。
异国情调的标记就这样被用来估量可变形的火车。现在火车又变成一个玩具机器人,浑身伤痕累累,盘坐在被闲置的支线上,读着摩门教的经典,心想这不就是一本被懒洋洋地重新讲述的圣经吗;这玩具机器人也很像一排正在锁定目标的肩扛式导弹,一触即发,随后又被折叠放回提箱里。在中国,没有人知道如何对付可变形的机器人,它紧盯着人满为患的火车,在远处滑行;并打算再次变回一列火车,或是驶向日本。变形机器人现在还原成一个人。可变形的人是孤独的。可变形的人把上下颠倒过来,去半岛上作短暂的游览。随后,他会回顾这段时光,并打算继续他的行程。他会忘记究竟发生了什么,他会认为它不过与他想要的、或不想要的东西有关。那也不是他的化油器,丰富的燃料和易燃的空气并未发生混合。

医疗惊悚

  这电影是关于那些开车或驾驶某种东西的人的故事。接近高热般狂乱,形状模模糊糊,事故现场传出碰撞的脆响,它没法再快了。剧场里的温控器指针轻晃在华氏103附近,银屏变得昏暗,幻觉产生了:我们都失去了宝贵的东西,比指甲还小的东西,我们必须爬来爬去寻找它。影院的地板越来越粘滑,将我们牢牢粘住,观众的挣扎安静下来,剩下的所有声音都汇集在大脑的脉冲里。它慢慢卷成鼓状物:当它下沉到意识深处,电影又开始抓紧它,晃动它。引座员在观众周围走来走去,一些人深受感染,被情节不幸地吞没了;而另一些人身体抽搐着,像个死结,接着飞炸成抗生素的榴霰弹。

(臧棣 译)

Nick Admussen

Road Trip

Convertible Car is now a train. Convertible Train has now become a Mormon by obeying commands in the secret ritual and it leaves on its holy mission. Its price in dollars becomes a price in yuan—fetish yuan, since one prefers recirculated air and closed compartments on most train tracks in China. Convertible Train is thus valued only according to its worth as an exotic emblem. Now it is becoming a robot, which is surprisingly painful, and it hunkers down on an unused spur line and reads the Book of Mormon and thinks this is just a lazily renarrated Bible and the banks of missiles in its shoulders keep deploying, locking on targets, and then folding back into its body. Nobody in China knows what to do with Convertible Robot and it watches trains crammed with people slide by in the distance and thinks of becoming a train again or moving to Japan. Convertible Robot is now a person. Convertible Person is alone. Convertible Person puts the top down and goes for a little jaunt down the peninsula, anyway. Later he will look back on this period and wonder what kept him moving along; he will have forgotten what it was, he will think it had to do with wanting or not wanting something and not his carburetor, mixing rich fuel with the tinder of the air.

Medical Thriller

This movie is about people driving cars or something. It gets a fever; the shapes blur, and in places where the action should be crisp, it can't quite get to speed. The theater's thermostat needle floats to 103 and the screen goes dark before the movie starts to hallucinate: we have all lost something invaluable and smaller than a fingernail and we must crawl around looking for it, the theater floor becoming stickier and stickier, gumming us down, the struggle of the audience going quiet and all remaining sound concentrated in the pulsing arteries of the brain. It is a slow roll of drumming: when it sinks in, the movie starts to seize and shake. Ushers swarm over the audience, some engulfing hapless and infected viewers, some throwing themselves into knots of twitching bodies, then exploding into antibiotic shrapnel.

托尼·巴恩斯通

毛发

昨天，我把冷水
泵进桶里，

泼在身上——
在雪国的庭院中洗澡，

郝特尔，一位年长的喇嘛，
在门庭那边观望，

他走过来，抓住一把
我的胸毛

使劲拽。
他从没见过这样的体毛，

我猜。我伸手去拉他
悬挂的胡须，

直拉得他大叫起来。
我们就这样了解对方。

跟他绝交（操作手册）

用削皮刀分开四肢和躯干，
然后像对付芒果一样削皮。
如果皮肤抗拒，就放在钝刀上，
来回摇，撬开。
肉体剥开后，就比较容易用细刀
在肌肉中来回拉锯，
然后切断筋，去掉脂肪。
现在，用一把钢斧头劈开主要关节，
像吃龙虾一样掰开骨头，
用小锤子敲破头骨，碎骨头和肉
混在一起。戴上塑料手套，和厚围裙。
然后等待秃鹰飞过来，

Tony Barnstone

Hair

Yesterday, as I pumped cold water
into a bucket

and poured it over myself
to bathe in the courtyard of the Snowlands

Hotel, an old monk, watching
from the porch,

came up to me, grabbed a handful
of my chest hair

and tugged it painfully.
He had never seen such body hair,

I suppose. I reached for one
of his hanging mustachios

and pulled it till he yelped.
In this way we understood each other.

Break Up with Him (A How-to Manual)

Score limbs and torso with a paring knife,
then peel just like a mango. If the skin
resists, to pry it up place a dull blade
beneath one edge and rock it back and forth.
With the meat flayed, it's easier to run
a slender blade between the muscles, then
to sever tendons and cut fat from flesh.
Now break the major joints with a steel hatchet,
crack bones as you would a lobster, crush
the skull with a small sledge and blend bone dust
with flesh. Wear plastic gloves, a heavy apron.
Then wait for turkey buzzards to wing in,

去啃笨拙的鸡腿肉，
伸一下脖子，瞪着你双眼发亮。

死亡

有一天你的脚趾脱落了，最小的脚趾，
右脚上那个。"我的脚趾！我的脚趾！"你哀悼，
"我最心爱的脚趾头！"紧接着你的大拇指也脱落，
还有一部分头发，和你的鼻子。你变形太快，
穿过人群时，人们惊吓地转过身来。
在一个红坐位酒吧里，一颗牙齿
掉进玻璃酒杯，起身时，一只耳朵
掉在假皮沙发上。接下来的实情是，
脱落加速：手臂二头肌，腿，
黑眼睫毛的眼睛，苍白肉色的嘴唇，头。
你家人来了，收拾残渣，
悲伤地为已死去的你唱歌，
然后把你种进肥沃的黑土地。
你飘浮在那里，在那个子宫里，等待分娩。

（明迪 译）

旧

他清理着衣箱，里面装满了
夏天的衣物。游泳衣，冲浪短裤，
泳镜，叠得整齐的沙滩衬衫，
全都洗过，被封好，装在塑料袋中。
可以看到一个丝滑的黑色胸罩，
紧身的运动短裤，漂亮时髦的黑上衣，
这一切对她已没有意义，似乎对他也是。
但她仍能像幽魂一样出没在他的睡眠中，
咬他的梦。他们曾如此亲近，他感到
她就像皮肤裹着他，他也像皮肤裹着她。
直到他们都被磨旧。当怀疑插足进来，她收敛起
她的爱，锁上箱子，离开了。似乎
他还能在一件女外套上嗅到她的某种气息。
哦不，它已洗过。洗得太干净，太干净。

（臧棣 译）

approach the flesh on clumsy chicken legs,
stretch their necks, watching you with burnished eyes.

Death

One day your toe fell off, the tiniest toe
on the right foot. "My toe! My toe!" you mourned,
"My favorite toe!" Your thumbs were next to go,
some hair, your nose. And you were so deformed,
you walked through crowds and people turned in fear.
And at the bar in a red booth, a tooth
dropped in your glass, and when you rose an ear
dropped on the naugahyde. And then in truth
the loss accelerated: biceps, legs,
your black-lashed eyes, your pale flesh lips, your head.
Your family came and gathered up the dregs,
and singing sadly for the you that's dead,
they planted you in the black fertile earth.
You float there in that womb and wait for birth.

Worn

He's cleaning out the trunk in which his clothes
are stored for summer, bathing suits, surf shorts,
swimming goggles, neatly folded beach shirts,
all laundered, put in plastic, and then closed
away—and finds a black and silky bra,
some short shorts with a tiny waist, a sleek
black top, all empty of her, as is he,
although she ghosts through him all night and gnaws
his dreams. They were so close he thought he wore
her like a skin, as she wore him till they
wore out. When doubt crawled in, she stored away
her love and latched the trunk and left. It seems
he catches just a whiff of her somewhere
in the blouse. No, it's clean. Too clean, too clean.

汴庭博

启程
为杜甫而作

大陆和岛屿间的凹陷里躺着海
她的黄昏子宫中无名的尖塔和森林
　　　　和山谷
和黑鲸和都市和酒瓮和骸骨
裸露着
在我们船下带条纹的航迹上拨弦
像踉跄高飞的陌生鸟儿。
当我前行,地貌变换着
海岸之上——梯地丰腴的斜坡
在无色的峰顶下,那郁郁葱葱的躯体
　　　　和枯燥的头
和大片夏季稍晚将变得阴暗的灌木丛。
此刻和那时,当一个人擦拭重重风尘并抛光
　　　　老旧的油漆
一个非时间的刷白的村子透出曙光,
它的冲天炉
和带旗帜的塔——好可爱,
　　　　可我仍是个陌生人被丢在这儿——
荧光微微而褪色像疲惫鸟儿正闭上的
亮眼睛。
泡沫喷过扎下的船头。
我转身,
风把海的容貌叠进古老逝去的线。
有我们幸福船坞的岛到了。

自最初的日子已有漂泊者,
那为何要哀怨?

(杨炼 译)

Breyten Breytenbach

Departure
(for Du Fu)

In the basin between mainland and island lies the sea
with in her twilight womb the unknown pinnacles and forests and valleys
and blackfish and cities and urns of wine and skeletons plucked bare
over which the track of our boat streaks
like the flight of a high strange staggering bird.
As I move forward, so the land changes face
above the coast—the terraced fertile slopes
under colourless mountain peaks are the lush bodies of arid heads
and bushes will be sombre this late in summer.
Now and then, as when one wipes layers of dust and varnish
from an old painting,
a timeless chalked village glimmers through, its cupolas
and towers with banners—lovely, but I still remain a stranger here—
glimmer and fade like the closing of a sleepy bird's shining eye.
Foam spurts past the plunging bow.
I turn around,
wind folds the sea's features into old lines of passing.
Already the island of our bliss slips a veil of mist over itself:

Since the oldest days there have always been travellers,
so why be sad?

波丽·克拉克

我的动物园学历

有一个规则我生而知之
从我呱呱坠地,我的嘴

那剧痛的、红艳的、新生的小洞,
未冒出牙齿的牙龈无用地张开。

我知晓这规则并殊死抵抗,
但蔓延的岁月中我不得不渐渐接受

那重量,我超常的体力就是
明证,当我十六岁

我能推着双轮车,堆满
颤颤悠悠的牛腰肉和鲜马肉

一口气推上山顶的狼穴。
惟有最威猛的壮汉才有这本事:

我听见笑声,还有别的,一种确认
除夕夜,当一年蜕变为

另一年的梦,他们吻我
一阵乱哄哄的,不安的吻。

亚马逊鹦鹉向我疾飞
我靠近他的窝就是一阵绿色的尖叫;

隔壁,凤头大鹦鹉逡巡踱步
他攀爬我,仿佛我是棵纠结的热带树

他的头探入我衬衣下的双乳间,
咕哝(你得侧耳倾听他的言语)

操你个母狗,他黄色的眼睛闪烁。
恐惧攫住我,我慌了,

Polly Clark

My Education at the Zoo

There is a rule which I am born knowing,
from the moment I slip out, and my mouth

becomes that anguished, red, newborn hole,
its ridge of unborn teeth uselessly bared.

I know this rule and am flailing against it.
But in later years I come to an uneasy acceptance;

my unusual physical strength is a testament
to its weight. When I am 16

I can push a barrow overflowing
with rolling cow haunch and pony carcass

all the way up the hill to the wolves.
Only the strongest of the strong men can do it:

there is laughter, and something else, a recognition.
On New Year's Eve, when one year metamorphoses

into a dream of another, they kiss me
with uneasy, snarling kisses.

The Amazon parrot whirls at me,
a green screech as I approach his nest.

Next door, the cockatoo is pacing up and down.
He clambers up me, as if I were a gnarled tropical tree,

lodges his head down my shirt between my breasts,
murmurs (you must incline your head to hear his words)

fuck you bitch, his yellow eyes blinking.
I'm afraid at the end I begin to fall apart,

一不小心放飞了三对情侣鸟
而凤头大鹦鹉,就坐在最近的树上

恶狠狠骂着脏话(突然间词语来了,
隐秘地,当我深夜时独自一人)。

真男人晌午时有种慵懒,像狮子
在骄阳下为自己蕴含着暴力。

入夜,连串的晚会上,我发现极难
不被指认或不泄漏真相。

我喝下十品脱啤酒,冷嘲一切辱骂,
拒绝退让,最后,在凌晨三点

狂笑爆发中,他们之间某一个
戴两只乳罩披件睡衣,粉墨登场

谁都欢呼他玩成了大赢家
这游戏的名称,现在我终于知道。

(杨炼 译)

成都按摩

我躺在那里整洁如一座英国村庄
当她的手指像冰雹刺痛我
她的拳头像雪球撞碎了我.
她拍打我,轻如一只鸭子
在爆炸般的指甲钉入
我的大腿之前——然后进入我的庙宇,
压得我眼冒金星——
我什么都看不见除了中国的
电子骨头,迷雾面孔
还有我自己巨大的沉默,堆砌盲目
讨厌以及固执如水泥

(翟永明 译)

and accidentally set three pairs of lovebirds free
and the cockatoo, who simply climbs the nearest tree

hurling insults (but suddenly the words begin to come,
secretly, when I am alone at night).

The real men bask at lunchtime, like lions keeping
their violence to themselves while the sun is hot.

At night, at party after party, I find it hard
to keep from being discovered or blurting the truth.

I drink ten pints, laugh at all insults,
refuse to retreat, as finally amidst howls

of laughter at 3 a.m., one of them emerges
wearing two bras and a nightie, his face covered in paint,

and everyone cheering his victory in the game
that he is playing, that now I know the name of.

Cheng Du Massage

I lie tidy as an English village
while her fingers sting me with sleet,
her snowball fists smash into me.
She pads around me, light as a coot,
before hammering exploding nails
into my thighs—then on to my temples,
pressing till my eyes spark—
and I see nothing but China's
electric bones, its face of fog—
and my own giant muteness, piled and blind,
unlovely and stubborn as cement.

我的生活，海

当我空虚的时候，
当我的生活极度贫瘠时：它包裹我
尽管我没有一物可以给它。
在我住过的旋转房间里它咆哮着，
那些跟随我的恋人们被它抓挠着
看他们都是用什么做成的，它退缩
当它发现他们浑身的黄金和热血。
那时我很软弱，我对自己的生活撒谎，
在我从岸边离开时它哭了，面目狰狞
呼吸酸涩。它发誓要一醉方休。
我对着天空和太阳张开嘴，
像鬼魂一样自由。我停止了交谈
把自己藏在人群和一种新的语言中。
有时候当我走过他们身边时电话响了
有时候信件找到我，被撕得支离破碎
我从不谈论我的生活而它也没有寻找我，
它睡在我的臂膀里像一条美丽的鱼。

（翟永明 译）

北 京

这城市在夜间大喘气，
一只猛兽，兽的雾虹霓。

白天它一边生长一边遗忘，
微若浮尘的人们穿过

它的臂膀，捡着奶头和牙齿。
在廉价的遗忘中，每一天

他们都在成百地沦丧。
我们在它伤痕累累的皮肤上旅行

直到一小块被擦破的天空
露出蔚蓝。我的眼睛一架起重机，

My Life, the Sea

There was a time when I was empty
and my life was ravenous: it lapped at me
though I had nothing to give it.
It yowled in the rolling rooms I inhabited,
it pawed the lovers who followed me there
to see what they were made of, recoiling
when it found them full of gold and blood.
I was weak and I lied to my life.
It sobbed at the shore as I left, its face ugly,
its breath sour. It swore to drink itself to death.
I opened my mouth to the sky and the sun.
I was free as a ghost. I stopped speaking.
I hid myself in crowds and a new language.
Sometimes phones would ring when I passed them.
Sometimes letters would reach me, torn into pieces.
I never spoke of my life and it did not find me,
except at night when I rolled wide awake
and it slept in my arms like a beautiful fish.

Beijing

At night the city exhales,
a beast of neon and fog.

By day it grows and forgets,
tiny people pick across

its shoulders, nipples and teeth.
Hundreds fall off each day

in an act of cheap forgetting.
We travel the scars of its skin

towards a sky scraped through
to the blue. My eyes a crane,

吊起那些脸，忽前忽后地
悠着。我觉得我熟悉他们，

那种机器模制的失神，
那演说着他们的工厂。

在我的头顶上方，建筑工们叮叮当当，
轮廓鲜亮的剪影如同孩子衬着太阳

这就是制造，制造，
我们的身体屈从的制造，

丧失的健忘，血的健忘，
古老的、无用的健忘，就像爱潮。

（唐晓渡 译）

天鹅

我以为就是你
一瞬间转身朝向我
从那失明的水中，

一个纯白的问号，
牵着它水下的梦
软化我脚边的石头。

我以为那就是你
假如不是你，
便是爱本身
完美地徐徐驶向我，

摇摆在自身的美当中，
水圈退散着
像人们不那么确信时的模样。

（周瓒 译）

I lift faces, swing them back
and forth. I feel I know them,

their machine-blankness,
the factory of their speech.

Far above me, builders clink,
sharp against the sun as children.

This is the making, making,
that our bodies are slave to,

forgetful of losses, of blood,
of ancient, useless waves of love.

Swan

I thought that it was you
turning to me for an instant
from the blindness of the water,

a pure white question
with its underwater dream in tow
softening the stones at my feet.

I thought that it was you
and if not you, then love itself
tacking perfectly towards me,

rocking in its own beauty,
the circles backing out
like people not quite believing.

女人

我航行到女人的世界,
乘一艘令她们毫无兴趣的宏伟船只。

我想象这就是爱她们:
把她们的记件活儿加起来,

苍白的颈项,鱼尾纹形的双足,
昂贵的嘴唇说着当然当然。

我已经学会了她们的语言,
我能说你以为如何?就像个本地人,

但她们不管,探察我的口音。
她们的目光越过红酒停在我身上。

她们的秘密如金钱般可感可触。
我们做买卖,于是我富了。我感到了自由。

我们比较歌声,比较我们腕子上的伤痕。
有时候我以为我已经找到了家。

当我拥有她们,我听到她们的骨头在哭叫。
她们昂贵的头发漂流着、闪耀着。

(周瓒 译)

Women

I sail into the world of women,
in a magnificent ship that does not interest them.

I imagine this is what loving them is:
adding up the piecework of them,

the pale neck, the sudden crow's feet,
the expensive lips saying *of course of course.*

I have learned their language, I can say
What do you think? like a native,

but they detect an accent in spite of me.
Their eyes rest on me over the wine.

Their secrets are palpable as money.
We trade and I grow rich. I feel free.

We compare songs, the cuts on our wrists.
Sometimes I think I have found my home.

When I hold them, I hear their bones crying.
Their costly hair drifts and shines.

与马共生

在知道有男人之前
我骑一匹无鞍的小马驰骋;
那是个艰难的冬天,但
我们是多么务实,决绝
在冰冷的空虚里,猛烈地跺着
冰,印下我们的姓名。

多年后我像马驹般卧在草地上,
渴望着触摸你的头发;
我们像阴影一样抓紧;
我的手指纠缠着往昔,亲吻
如父母之吻般热切的吞咽,
飞奔,什么也挡不住我。

今夜我穿上衣服
像一个秘密;你会看到
我的臂肘像马趾般伸出,
我小心翼翼剪断我的鬃毛的样子,
我的双眼由于害怕你而转动的模样吗?
我正试着藏起动物的我;

而你给我一条项链,
明亮如一只马嚼子,你还把
你的名字印刻
在大地上,我的胳膊
绕着你,无力得像一条缰绳,
没有什么能够阻止我,
不再有母亲或父亲。

(周瓒 译)

My Life with Horses

Before I knew there were men
I galloped a pony bareback;
It was a hard winter, but
how sure-footed we were, resolute
in frozen emptiness, stamping
the ice with our names.

Years later I lay like a foal in the grass,
wanting to touch your hair.
We clutched like shadows,
I twined the past through my fingers, kissing
great gulps of father, of mother,
galloping with nothing to stop me.

Now in the evening I put on my dress
like a secret; will you see
how my elbow pokes like a hock,
the way I have carefully cut my mane,
the way my eyes roll from fear of you?
I'm trying to hide the animal I am.

And you give me a necklace,
bright as a bit, and you're
stamping your name
into the earth, and my arm
is around you, weak as a halter,
and nothing can stop me, no mother or father.

简妮芬·克劳馥

回旋
隐含的记忆

这两只丝鸟被磨损而后它触摸他们。
这两只破损的丝之鸟。在河里潜泳和浮现。
如是之丝绽裂河之石而这是它的丝水面,
它时间的绿水面织在丝时间里,它的水。
你能以精确的撕裂切下你的脚。若你能察觉。
你把手放在它上面抚摸那锋利
感知在手里。丝鸟们俯冲
沿着攀上悬崖尽头的灰色小径的枝叶,
他们下来饮水。他们飞
越过劈开悬崖穿过岩石切至水的根
视觉极慢又太快。且循序加速。
这里,当河床裸着身子软下来,
在此进入水之记忆,进入恍如未来之水的
倾角。这些形式永不会完成。
以他们全方位的压力,热与声。
进来攥在一起,进来烘干和漂浮。
潜入即全然纳入彼此的粒子中,攥牢或漂浮。

(杨炼 译)

Jennifer Crawford

a tempo
      (implicit memory)

these two silk birds are frayed and then it touches them.
these two frayed silk birds. into the river diving and emerging.
one such silk is a cracked river stone and this is the surface of its silk,
the green surface of its time in that silk time, its water.
you could cut your foot on that accurate division. if you weren't aware.
you could lay your hand on it and feel the sharpness
aware in your hand. these silk birds come down
from the leaves of the grey way up on the edge of the cliff,
they come down to the water to drink. they fly
past the roots that break the cliff and through the stone cuts water.
absolutely slowly and too fast to see. so holds acceleration in array.
where, when the riverbed bares its posture and then softens,
there go into the memory of water, into the likely inclination
of future water. and these forms will get undone.
by their full registration of pressure, heat and sound.
into holding together, into dry and adrift.
the dive is whole into each particle, held or adrift.

安东尼·邓恩

跳蚤马戏团

时间一到我们便将大帐篷打包，
装进货车车厢而后驶出地图。

回到黑暗中这玻璃帐篷恢复了活力：
秋千与大炮，跳水池以及高高的铁丝网，

样样东西震动着一场狂暴的表演。
尽管我们过后会归咎于——大打出手——

我们从不确定我们中的哪一个
丢下未钩好的帐篷而去；由于欺诈或疏忽

使我们的明星伺机逃逸，以一个利落的
跳跃穿过后备箱里数不清的无门。

但它们逃掉了，无疑，当我们到达。
尽管我们将状况处理到最好，一派兴旺，

且发现我们自己熟练于微型机械学，
我们中的一些人憎恨依赖小把戏为生

并感到在我们不满的痒痒中
我们伟大希望的飞翔之咬啮，流血。

一生的滴滴排水沟渐渐浅显。
而跳蚤们，不知怎的，仍然，惹怒我们。

(周瓒 译)

蝴蝶专家

他想解开她的白大褂
看她能变成什么；

一根手指划过蝶翼
白绸上他辉煌的设计——

Antony Dunn

Flea Circus

When the time came we packed up the Big Top,
stowed it in the trunk and drove off the map.

Back in the dark the glass tent came alive:
trapeze and cannon, plunge-pool and high-wire,

everything shaken to a frenzied show.
And though we'd later accuse—come to blows—

we'd never be sure which of our number
left the Top unhooked; by trick or blunder

let our stars seize the chance, make a clean jump
out through the countless non-doors of the trunk.

But fled they were, for sure, when we arrived.
And though we made the best of it, and thrived,

found ourselves skilled in micro-mechanics,
some of us resented living off tricks

and felt in the itch of our bad-feeling
the bite of our great hope's flight, the bleeding,

the drop-by-drop drain of a life gone thin.
The fleas, somehow, still, get under our skin.

Lepidopterist

He'd like to unfold her from that lab-coat
and see what kind of creature she'd become;

chalk up a finger on a butterfly-wing
and lay out his great design on white silk—

一条无重的裙子；擦光
她裹着黑粉和红色的皮肤上

他的指纹；看，她移行
横过店堂，盒子弹开

每一只蝴蝶脱钩而
抛自己于空中，而悬定。

他想让胸中结茧的东西
停止翻滚——自他口中爆开

难言的翅膀。他想说些什么
她能懂，却抓不住。

(杨炼、有玲 译)

未说的话

过后还会有时间。
而现在，找我们的路就已足够
穿过随浪退下的乌贼和海星
遍布的狗鲨骸骨被漂白
从尾到头，那没有眼睛的头，那些爪子，
那些腿，那些空空如也的蟹壳；
所有这一切足以让我们释怀；
摇晃着穿过这石头的潮汐
穿过防波堤和鱼笼中
海鸥还没来得及光顾的吃食；
知道百页云的太阳会
再来，还会再来，而我们
仍能彼此认出。让我们
把那些不得不说的话省着。
过后有的是时间。

(唐晓渡 译)

a dress for her to wear weightlessness in;
or dust his fingerprints across her skin

in kohl and carmine; or see, as she moves
through the store-room, the cases fly open

and every last butterfly unhook itself
and throw itself into the air, and stay.

He'd like the creature cocooned in his chest
to stop turning over—to burst from his mouth

on unspeakable wings. He'd like to say something
that she'd understand, but can't pin it down.

Unsaid

There will be time for this later.
Just now, though, let it be enough
to find our way through the backwash
of cuttlefish and brittlestars,
the yards of dogfish spine, stripped white
from tail to eyeless head, the claws,
the legs, the gutted hulls of crabs;
to be undone by all of this;
to roil across this tide of stones
through all the gulls have left undone
among the groynes and landing traps;
to know the shuttered sun will come
again, will come again, that we
still make each other out. Let's say
that what we have to say we'll save.
There will be enough time later.

威廉·赫伯特

仲夏灯之夜塔

一，
冬天，老高光灯塔说着
海风的语言
和雹子：冷解开自己，一片
接一片，绕着抽泣的边沿。

春天，它又一次发现阳光，
从它铅皮遮盖的眼球
云朵飞散如鸥鸟，大地的风喃喃
贴紧塔内的平台，口吃而锐利。

但在夏日迟暮和黑暗中它吐露
自己的方言：猝然如一口楼梯的深井
寂静如一条门廊，当灯的开关
一抖，它教我如何去听。

二，
你想，这音乐自何方响起，
它来自渔船的桅杆和绷紧
绳索的撞击，马达的呼噜波荡
像河面上一轮臃肿的月亮滴淌
或卸下的鱼篓，声声砸向码头？

你想，这音乐在何处合成自己？
当一年即将翻转进入此夜，
它像块巨大的透镜斜斜撑着楼板；
它像条鳐鱼浮上水面晒暖自己
侧身沉落时眼睛闪闪发光。

三，
就这样我们翻译寂静
死者再次开口：聆听
空空的大气用被梦碾碎的家庭们
充溢两个多世纪的房间：
就这样用他们的脸攥紧皱纹，
就这样平衡于他们的呼吸间。

W.N. Herbert

A Midsummer Light's Nighthouse

1
In Winter the Old High Light speaks
the language of the sea winds
and the hail: cold unwraps itself, sheet
after sheet, around its weeping edge.

In the spring it rediscovers sunlight,
lets the clouds peel off like gulls
from its lead-lidded eyeball. The earth wind mouths
against the landing door, yammering and keen.

But in the simmer-dim and dark it talks
in its own dialect: sudden as a stairwell
and silent as a corridor when the light-switch
flicks, it tells me how to listen.

2
Where do you think the music comes up from,
manifested in the taut ropes ringing
off masts of fishing boats, the grunt of motors rippling
like a fat moon's dribble on the river
and the knocking tread that's boxes, dropped upon the quays?

Where do you think the music groups itself
before the year turns over in the night?
It's propped against these timbers like a giant lens;
it's like a sunfish that's warmed itself in top waters
the eye flashing as it rolls away and drops.

3
It is by how we translate silence that
the dead become retongued—listen to
this empty air that fills two centuries
and more of chamber with the dreaming crush
of families: how it holds the creases in
their faces; how it's poised between their breaths.

四，
让舰队司令倾斜着滑离
他的基座，从鸟粪覆盖的大理石移向
雪白的海象群，一条悠游的小白鲸，
他的船笛吹奏古老灾难的
金丝雀之歌，战争消溶在水上。

让走私的女人在她的海蜇衬裙中
来到，缎带缠结着儿子们，
用罗姆酒调浓的毒液抹墙，
用陈年烟草的音色哼哼一首抓丁队蓝调，
她的迎迓对开如冷冰冰的双腿。

五，
海不在秋天分娩
像果园——它退落
像捻起翻动的一页
我们读它的休止，风平浪静。

于是意念施展权力
截断故事，在窗台上平衡我们
趁这条河还未清扫净钟声
还未将又一个夏至葬入海底。

让迎着我们汹涌的生命，
像午夜的嘀嗒之前一道横亘的裂缝：
此后是我们住不进的空虚，
这高高的光是我们共同的家。

(杨炼 译)

庇护雌狐

一扇旧推拉窗洞开的吠叫
高高在午夜的大街之上
可令她蹒跚着退却
穿过柏油碎石路面的脚爪咔嗒。
我本可留神看那巡航舰
灯光的临时村落，河流
使它们沉迷的欢宴
变成北海缓慢的神经突触。

4
Let the admiral slither from
his pedestal, turned from guanoed marble to
white walrus, a crawling beluga,
and pipe in his ship-whistle voice canary songs
of old calamities, wars dissolving on water.

Let the smuggler woman come
in her jellyfish petticoats, ribbons fouled with sons,
smearing the walls with rum-thickened venom,
and slur in old tobacco tones her press-gang blues,
her welcoming couplets like cold thighs.

5
The sea does not bring forth in Autumn
like an orchard—it draws back
like a page that's pinched for turning.
We read in it abeyance, not a swell.

Therefore the mind exerts its right
to halt the story, poise us on this sill
before the river sweeps the chimes away
and buries yet another solstice out at sea.

These other lives that surged before us,
let them be the gap before this midnight's tick:
our own no more inhabitable void succeeds it,
and the High Light is our common home.

Shields Vixen

An old sash window's opening bark
high above the midnight street
may have caused her limping retreat
across the claw-click of the tarmac.
I'd looked out to see the cruise ship's
instant village of lights, the river
letting their consuming revelry
become the sea's slow northerly synapse.

相反我呆立在那里，观望她：
一面钠的罗网过滤的带沙毛皮，
双肩颤动在我的凝视中；
但心灵滑过它的防波堤，
血液乱撞于我的喉咙——
她那特别的，已带不走的红。

(周瓒 译)

泰恩河隧道

这些天我特地调整频率
当我接近隧道，盼着收听
女高音，钢琴的装饰颤音，
色彩纷呈，当我付完钱并摇上
我的车窗，把车灯调成近光
接着驶向河流的腹地。

静电涌来，相当从容：
它把自己停靠在这歌声，弦乐演奏者一边，
发出嘘声，急促流动，窒息，下沉，
然后它统治一切好似耳中的毒药，
别的交通拥堵，刮擦和拖动——
铁罐子经过岩石，泥沙穿过鱼鳃：峡谷。

我总感到它会被某首
歌干扰，一支你只会在
这下面听到的歌闯入：这舌头
被挤压，一半火腿，一半雅纳切克；
这消息寒冷，迸发，毁坏——
但直到阳光出现啥也没发生，渐渐地，

同一支曲子因水的重力而改变。

(周瓒 译)

Instead I froze there, watching her:
fur filtered sandy by a sodium gauze,
shoulders twitching under my gaze;
and mind slipped past its breakwater,
blood thrummed in my throat—
the very red she'd gone without.

Tyne Tunnel

These days I tune in specially
as I approach the tunnel, hoping for
sopranos, pianistic flourishes,
colouristic passages, as I pay and wind
my window up, switch on dipped lights
and descend to the river's underbelly.

The static comes in swells, quite leisurely:
it pulls itself over the voice, the strings,
it shushes, couries, smothers, sinks,
and then it reigns like poison in the lug,
a crush of other traffic, a scrape and drag—
cans across rock, silt through gills: the gully.

I always feel it will be troubled by
some voice that breaks in with a song
you only hear down here: the tongue
compressed, half-ham, half-Janáček;
the message cold, eruptive, wrecked—
but there's nothing till sunlight and, gradually,

the same tune altered by the weight of water.

原谅苍蝇

必须原谅苍蝇
因为它们如此年轻,
它们的脑皮质这样孱弱,
以致弄不懂
它们爬过的都是些什么。
它们向万物礼敬
如同礼敬众神:
糖和屎对它们
同是甘美的点心。
神经质的愉悦
令它们呕吐,并误解
我们卷起的报纸,
以为我们致命的一挥
不过是依依惜别时的致意。

(唐晓渡 译)

鬼　魂
马歇尔·斯文尼的主题变奏

鬼魂不认道但必须回家
穿过大白天它在荒漠中绊了一跤
并摸索隐在黑暗中的通道。
它在地图上累满卵石以卜占
冬日翻过大平原的路径。
它在湖水中自沉以触摸
白桦根系的感受,它坐进
绵羊和山羊们的身体,
它们的血消融不了彻骨的寒意。
夏日多脂的空气中,它
在蚊虫之间旅行,
如同一本朽烂之书的原文
它在剥落的树皮中把自己裹紧。
它只知道向北,结果是
月复一月地朝着一个错误的方向行进。
有时它以为能辨认出
三角叶杨的造型

Forgive the Flies

We must forgive the flies
because they are so young,
their cortices so small,
that they don't understand
what it is they crawl on.
They greet everything
like little deities:
sugar and excrement
are each as good to them.
They vomit in their nervous
pleasure and mistake
our rolled up newspapers,
suppose our dying hands
are merely waving back.

Ghost
(Variation on a theme by Matthew Sweeney)

The ghost which doesn't know its way but must get home
stumbles in the desert through the day
and searches through the passes in the dark.
It gathers pebbles into maps to guess at its passage
across the great steppe in winter.
It immerses itself in lakes to feel
what the birch roots feel, it sits
in the bodies of sheep and goats
whose blood can't halt the chill.
It travels from mosquito to mosquito in
the fat summer air,
it wraps itself up in fallen trees' bark
like the text in a rotten book.
It only knows North and consequently
may be travelling in the wrong direction for months.
Sometimes it thinks it recognises
a configuration of poplars

于是一种巨大的疑惧降临。
它与蛆和粪便打成一片
一长排蹲坑,臭气熏陷刀城。
它记得那些见过的脸,却没想过
初见即是永别。记忆被缩减
而且必须像念珠被一一清点:
那老女人喉咙里的棘轮,
那现已失名的机场里
廉价小报的气味,
那神经质地拉上窗帘的手,
那婴儿黑瞳仁闪亮的一瞬。

   (唐晓渡 译)

祖父母

当你在梦中见到他们
他们似乎并未死去
你的安慰还是会被猛地扯痛
好像他们仍在生长
如同你曾经的那样:二十尺、三十尺
对一个家,太高太大,站着
像一群灯柱,一群马,一群电报杆,
合伙加入死亲戚的森林,
红杉的祖先,你在梦的忧伤中奔跑
直到抓住他们的腿
而他们试着
弯下腰,用无微不至的
巨大关怀,够你。

   (唐晓渡 译)

边界母牛

一头母牛正在夕照中撒尿:
一头黑母牛,在棕色和白色的
姐妹丛中,目光穿过重重山丘
直达边界,尽管她对此懵然不晓。
一根操纵杆沿着它的脊背延展,
有什么被陡地抓紧
尾巴倏然翘起,脖根堆满皱折。

and a great dread descends.
It lies with the maggots and the excrement beneath
a row of toilet stalls in Knife City.
It remembers faces seen with no thought that this was for
the last time. Memories are diminished
and must be counted out like beads:
the ratchet in the old woman's throat,
the smell of cheap newsprint in
a now nameless airport,
the hand nervously gathering a curtain,
the baby's black button blink.

Grandparents

When you meet them in dreams
as though they hadn't died
your comfort still feels wrenched.
It's like they continued to grow
as you grew: twenty, thirty feet
tall, too big for home, standing
like lampposts, horses, telegraph poles,
gathered into forests of dead relatives,
redwood ancestors, where you run
to clutch their legs in the dream's distress
while they attempt to
bend and reach you with
their careful huge caress.

Border Cow

A cow is pissing in the twilight:
a black cow, in a field of brown and white
sisters, looking across the hills
to the border, though she doesn't know this.
She has a cord that runs along her back
which something has seized abruptly,
rodding her tail up, runkling her neck.

尿流滚滚，微微闪光，
那气味似乎为黄昏平添了星星点点的脏，
它把母牛和草地焊在一起，
是一个锐角，而不是曲线。
这母牛斜倚着的尿液
闪烁如一支独角鲸的长牙，一根狼牙棒，
据此她好像缓解了她的紧张。

　　（唐晓渡 译）

慢动物穿行

狐猴们以某种方式，在路的轻快处
向上并侧身于树林间，俯身穿过
去德里贝村途中的农场。
当然，有些更慢的生物也能穿行：
乌龟以庄严、擦拭的步履
或者树懒，游得彷佛下沉
也不失颜面，这样的气水肺会被
诱捕进它们蓬乱的蜘蛛毛。
我想到水因为那天晚上满是水
还有白蛙跳进我的光
好像在嚼口香糖并试图
从跑道上逃出来。我也想到狐猴
每当我看见那个因为夜
而成为红字的标志，还有三个人
走回家的故事，左边那人
对什么人说"晚安"，而
右边那个对另外的人说"晚安"
还有中间那个问他们
跟谁说话？一个看见了男的
另一个看见了女的，两个人都
描述了第三人的父母，转入
去墓地的道路。当我想起
狐猴时我已忘了它们的名称
来自拉丁文的精灵，我只看见
穿过夜路慢慢爬行在我心里
回到我父母家和我女儿的
那些狐猴的土匪眼和斑纹尾和软灰脊背
和白手，精致地放置在
路的扭曲和耸肩处。

Her stream gleams thickly as
the air gains evening's soot-smuts:
it strings her to the grass
at a strict angle, no curve,
just the liquid she leans against
gleaming like a narwhal's tusk, an ashplant,
as she strains to be relieved.

Slow Animals Crossing

Lemurs somehow, at that lilt of the road
up and sideways at the trees, stooping through
the farmyard on the way to Derrybeg.
Surely there are slower creatures who could cross:
turtles with their solemn wiping gait
or sloths who swim as though to sink
is no disgrace, such aqualungs of air would be
trapped among their matted spider hair.
I think of water since that night was full of it
and white frogs leapt into my lights
like chewing gum attempting
to free itself from tarmac. And I think of lemurs
whenever I see that sign with its red letters
because of the night, and the story
of the three men walking home, and the man
on the left said "goodnight" to someone, and
the man on the right, "goodnight" to someone else
and the man in the middle asked who
were they talking to? And one had seen a man
and one had seen a woman, and both
described the third man's parents, turning off
at the road to the graveyard. And when I thought
of lemurs I'd forgotten they were named
for the Latin word for spirits, and I only saw,
crawling slowly in my mind across the night road
back to my parents' house and my daughter,
the bandit eyes and banded tails and soft grey backs
and the white hands of lemurs, delicately placed
upon the twist and the shrug of the road.

桑蒂尼科坦

在昏暗的水泥门厅跟德邦简的女教授
坐在折椅上静静闲聊在
越来越沉默的树下,但没有暗到
我看不见高处的树枝和蝙蝠
更暗的蓝叶翅投在涌动的蓝乳汁上
在沉默无星的天空里,一个空间处于
每个词和它的近邻之间越来越长
像一个城镇变成乡村直到
我们走回家沿着大道
有巨树我看见某人
在田野里抽烟,现在暗得只有
他们冰冷的烟头在
站在树枝下的桌前
修理路人衣裳的裁缝另一边
但还有另一个,也许在跳舞
或懒懒挥动着成为我第一批
萤火虫然后还有
它们不确定的一团团,萤火虫一直
回往宽阔的运河边直到
我们遇到一群人用绳子
拉紧在弯道上打滑而
翻倒在路肩并把所有泥块
撒到草地上的卡车而
看起来我们也应该拉住
腕粗的绳子如今在漆坛般的黑暗里
直到我们无法说出但能感觉到那辆
近乎决断的、倾斜卡车的沉着
然后它用如此的决心回撞
以致把我们抛回
我们各自的方向而
德邦简和我继续去普朗迪克
全然不知那折断脖子的可怜司机
鬼魂来和我们一起往回吹并喝下
蜜糖威士忌再听我们闲聊
还躺在我房间空余的床上
看天花板吊扇的棕色叶片
慢慢转到停息。

(杨小滨 译)

Santiniketan

Dark on the concrete porch with Debanjan's professor
in a deckchair chatting quietly beneath
the increasing silence of the trees, but not so dark
I couldn't see the high branches and the bats'
darker blue blades against the welling blue milk
of the silent starless sky, the space between
each word and its neighbour growing longer
like a town becoming countryside until
we were walking home along the avenue
of huge trees and I saw someone
smoking in the field, so dark now it was just
the cold tip of their cigarette just beyond
where the tailor had stood with his table below
the branches to repair the passers-bys' clothing
but there was another, dancing perhaps
or waving lazily becoming my first
fireflies—and then there were
uncertain constellations of them, fireflies all the way
back beside the broad canal until
we came upon a crowd with ropes
taut by the bend where the truck had slipped
and fallen on one shoulder spilling all
its earthy rubble on the lawn and
it seemed as though we too should haul on
the wrist-thick ropes in pitcher darkness now
until we couldn't tell but felt the poise
of the almost-decided, half-right truck
and then it thudded back with such
determination that it threw us all
back in our separate directions and
Debanjan and I went on to Prantik
never knowing that the broken-necked poor driver's
ghost came blowing back with us and drank
molasses whisky and listened to us chat
and lay upon the spare bed in my room
and watched the ceiling fan's brown blades
spin slowly to cessation.

一匹很难的马

一匹马向外注视着海
从不远处倾斜的田野
在阿伯丁镇外。我在
前往邓迪的火车上观察它。
它是静止的,在我看见它的
那一分钟里注视着。
它是一匹小棕马,
甚至可能是幼驹。
海是宁静的。马
看着像个老渔夫,
甚至可能是条老鱼。
很难想象它会
动。很难知道
它在想什么。
它是一匹很难的马。

(杨小滨 译)

A Difficult Horse

The horse is staring out to sea
from a sloping field not far
out of Aberdeen. I watch it from
the train to Dundee.
It is stationary, staring for
the minute I have it in view.
It is a small brown horse,
possibly even a pony.
The sea is calm. The horse
looks like an old fisherman,
possibly even an old fish.
It's difficult to imagine it ever
moving. It's difficult to know
what it is thinking.
It is a difficult horse.

肖恩·奥布莱恩

城市

还需朝下走

城市由什么构成？排气孔。蓝光。谋杀。
从幽暗到幽暗，一步步走下来，
走过直奔焦渴灯盏的黄色头盔，走过棉衣
狗熊般哀戚地比划着，表达着常见
却无望的说不清的爱，走过男人
和他们的发式、他们的瞥眼、未出口的建议。
都知道，这无论是谁肯定已经死去。
那被取走的、无眼的、煮过的器官——千般状态
等待着被发现，被哀悼，被排列在
犯罪者发臭的象征物收藏中间：
剪下的指甲、指骨、鼠毛、牛奶
一本古书枯黄的纸页间夹着
钥匙或答案。但你继续朝下走
时间伸展，办公室里的钟表
绷着劲，歇斯底里地相互盯看。
你的同事们在日光的世界里
玩帆船喝啤酒一小时，打绝望的哈欠。
但你继续下降直到你离开
秩序的最后边卡，远远后移的地界，
这里铸铁楼梯已让位于木地板。
想在此停步，将铅的手提箱
倾倒一空，将此地变成乌有之乡？
楼梯自动折叠而起
寂静的隧道进一步推进
上面是伸展的铁轨路基、瓶装的河流、
牡蛎贩子的墓地、泥瓦匠的图书馆、建设者的公厕、
食肉的摩洛克魔王那窗玻璃脏兮兮的教堂、
遮光窗扇、走廊、碗柜、盒子。
坐下，你的手电筒画着砖墙
见涂鸦咕哝出老哑嗓——"好像是亚拉姆语"——
听着寂静喘息这是这是这是，
一部粗麻布和尘土做成的大书
无止境地合着，阅读它自己——

Sean O'Brien

Cities

'and still some down to go'
    (Ken Smith)

What are cities made of? Steam vents. Blue light. Murder.
Steps going down from the dark to the dark
Past yellow helmets aiming anxious lamps, past padded coats
Making sorrowing bearlike gestures of general
But hopelessly inarticulate love, past men
And their haircuts, their eyebeams, unspoken advice.
Everyone knows. Whoever it is must already be dead.
Eviscerated, eyeless, boiled—in a thousand conditions
They wait to be found and lamented, chained
Amid the perpetrator's stinking hoard of symbols:
Nail-clippings, fingerbones, rat hair, milk,
Scorched pages of an ancient book
That holds the key. But down you go
And the hours stretch, and the clocks in the offices
Stare at each other in rigid hysteria.
Your colleagues in the daylight world
Yawn with despair, an hour from sailboats and beer.
But you go on descending until you have left
The last outpost of order some far landing back
Before cast-iron stairs gave way to wood.
Isn't it tempting to dump the aluminium suitcase
And stop here, making a place of this nowhere?
The staircase folds back on itself
And the silent tunnel plunges further in
Under the last of the railbeds, the last bottled river,
Graveyard of oystermen, library of masons, latrine of the founders,
Stained-glass temple of carnivorous Morlocks,
Deadlight, corridor, cupboard, box.
Sit with your torch playing over the brickwork
Still hoarse with graffiti—"*looks like Aramaic*"—and listen
To the silence breathing *This is and this is and this is,*
Endlessly folding and reading itself,
A great book made of burlap and dust,

它的滴水和沙沙声、来自旧案件的尖叫、
上世纪驶向另一个地方的
火车。很快你就会相信
你已吃下了部本书，
你的食道像一间条状出租屋污迹满满，
你的舌头会给出说明
你的呼吸会有牙髓的气味。
是否想说，告诉我原因
我们就上去透气——那地上已是黎明
锅炉的检修孔张开，复苏的
蒸汽直上蓝天
我们在那里寻求释怀——上到那里
并将这一切再一次统统忘记。

(西川 译)

欧洲人

我们这是在欧洲我们得
喜欢路边的蘑菇摊，
这宽边盘子和制服纽扣般的蘑菇
黎明前采自桦树林，
这阴湿的美味的单腿肉身
爬上深如森林大如森林的
墓坑，无需花时间
发展顾客，无需花时间
忘记当初，无需花时间
抱着满桶或满筐的蘑菇
唠家常，耸肩
以证明我们的知识和我们的无知
合乎身份，众所周知，完全
超乎历史或法律的范围，
既然我们总在这里
靠近十字路口，坐着折叠椅，
臃肿地穿着黑外套，苍白如我们的产品，
寻找和贩卖大地之肉
论把论斤装进棕黄色的纸袋子，
我们活的真是无比真实。

(西川 译)

That is simply digesting the world—
Its drips and rustles, the screams from old cases,
Trains that were heading elsewhere
In a previous century. Soon
You will come to believe you have eaten this book,
That your gullet is lined like a tenement room with its print,
That your tongue has illustrations
And your breath must smell of pulp.
Isn't it tempting to answer, *Just give me the reason*
And then we'll go up to the air—it is dawn above ground
And the manholes stand open, steaming
For the resurrection, straight up in the blue
Where we seek reassurance—*go up there*
And start to forget it all over again.

Europeans

Now we are in Europe let us take
To selling mushrooms by the roadside,
Broad-brimmed platefuls and uniform buttons
Plucked before dawn in the forest of birch,
The dank delicious one-legged flesh
Climbing from grave-pits as big and as deep
As the forests themselves, for it does not
Take long to establish the custom, not long
To forget the beginning, to hold up
A bucket or basket of mushrooms
And talk about always and offer a shrug
That proves our knowledge and our ignorance
Identical, proverbial, entirely
Beyond the scope of history or law,
And since we have always been here
On our fold-away chairs near the crossroads,
Hunched in black overcoats, pale as our produce,
Seeking and selling the flesh of the earth
By the handful and kilo in brown paper bags,
We cannot be other than real.

桌和椅

> "无辜之墙与光"
> ——罗伊·弗勒

桌和椅,"无辜之墙与光",
离了我们哪儿都不在。步入这房子,
田野边上,两条没编号的路交汇,
又沿着银桦树山脊分开。
镜子和首饰残留着尘封
空气的微嘘;照片上的人物
从市政厅台阶上微笑疑惑地
回顾。那些曾是日子。
而这些是什么?这些寂静
不会被我们的言谈或手势
或常则甚或爱打断,从未
辍止从黑暗陨落向黑暗?
见证一只盥洗壶的忧伤
我们能收回什么?
站进一个老石水槽,
它像只忠实专注的狗?如果
我们该深究一块遗落在
窗台上的瓦釉的开片,再
模拟窗户那壁立之目
瞪视日常的空,院子,大门
微启,领我们回到起点
又觑着我们游离出此地,
我们以为还能寻得多少残余的
耐力,在命定与机遇之间?

(杨炼 译)

Tables and Chairs

> "the innocent walls and light"
> (Roy Fuller)

The tables and chairs, "the innocent walls and light",
Would be nowhere without us. Enter this house
At the edge of a field, where two unnumbered roads
Converge and part across a ridge of silver birch.
The mirrors and the ornaments survive
The almost-hush of the unopened air; the figures
In the photographs look back in smiling disbelief
From the Town Hall steps. Those were the days.
So what are these, these silences that never cease
To fall between darkness and darkness,
That we cannot interrupt with speech
Or gestures or routine or love? What shall we gain
By witnessing the pathos of a ewer
Standing in an old stone sink,
As faithful and attentive as a dog? If we should
Scrutinize the cracked glaze of a tile
Left lying on the window-sill, and then pass on
To emulate the windows' wall-eyed stare
At ordinary emptiness, a yard, the gate
Ajar to take us back where we began
And see us off the premises,
What margin of endurance do we think
We'll find, between necessity and chance?

另一个国家

"能去那儿就去吧"——奥登

解散的同志们,记起办公室的罐头被某人偷了,
那是我们为赢不了罢工的矿工募集的。

某人偷了特纳,上衣,又傻笑着走开,
谁干了这事儿,我们咒你成个渴鬼。

你为一切对南边儿的厌恨撑腰——
那贪婪,势利,不停讥讽的嘴角

要问啥造出一盘散沙?唯有——我,
确切无疑,你总是个世界的适者。

北方?另一国。你认识的人从没去过。
巴特珊格,斯诺当,梯尔曼斯通:在哪儿?在肯特。

"人民"今天说这些看法吓人的不公,
但宽宥的此"人民"已非彼"人民"。

现在你霜鬓的孩子笑笑耸肩:"那是历史"。
那么为昔日大发感叹有什么意思"?

每当某人一本正经说该画条线了,
我们就猜到银子都被他们提走了。

战火整年爆发之处,有"风景"有牌匾,
可纵然你深埋那东西,它依旧会回返:

这里倒下又一场英国内战的伤亡者,
某人,某时刻——你,或许——将不得不负责。

(杨炼 译)

Another Country

"Get there if you can"
    —Auden

Scattered comrades, now remember: someone stole the staffroom tin
Where we collected for the miners, for the strike they couldn't win,

Someone stole a tenner, tops, and then went smirkingly away.
Whoever did it, we have wished you thirsty evil to this day:

You stand for everything there was to loathe about the South—
The avarice, the snobbery, the ever-sneering mouth,

The lack of solidarity for any cause but *me*,
The certainty that what you were was what the world should be.

The North? Another country. No one you knew ever went.
(Betteshanger, Snowdown, Tilmanstone: where were they? In Kent.)

"People" tell us nowadays these views are terribly unfair,
But these forgiving "people" aren't the "people" who were there.

These days your greying children smile and shrug: *That's history.*
So what's the point of these laments for how things used to be?

Whenever someone sagely says it's time to draw a line,
We may infer that they've extracted all the silver from the mine.

Where all year long the battle raged, there's "landscape" and a plaque,
But though you bury stuff forever, it keeps on coming back:

Here then lie the casualties of one more English Civil War,
That someone, sometime—you, perhaps—will have to answer for.

帕斯卡尔·帕蒂

我父亲的身体

当我坐在这儿握着你的手
确信你曾是个强奸犯,
我觉得仅仅缩制你的头
是多么不够。
我可以缩制你的整个身体
用我作为一名雕塑家学到的技艺。
我会用火山的热力,
火焰河的水波
以及火焰河床上的热沙
我要对着这些材料唱歌。
它们会答唱,闪着辉光。
即使黑瓦洛的人头猎手
也会震惊于我是多么容易地
剥开你脖子上的皮
并一直向下撕到你的双脚。
我如何将你的肉丢给
我的动物们
要是它们饿了。
巨蟒独木舟将载着
你的器官去往那盛宴
而我要缝好你的裂缝。
然后我会煮你的皮
用河流的火焰把它熨平。
我会用热沙填充你身体的袋子,
丑恶将咕嘟咕嘟涌出去。
我不会停手
直到你被缩制到足以充当我的玩偶。
我会把你挂在一只钩子上
我瞪眼看我赤裸的爸爸
你那根微型阴茎
连一只耗子都伤害不了。
我会把你带到森林的某处
那里只有小孩子们允许去。
我在那里漫步,要听听
你的灵魂都说过什么。

Pascale Petit

My Father's Body

As I sit here holding your hand
knowing that you were once a rapist,
I think how it isn't enough
just to shrink your head.
I could shrink your whole body
with the skills I learnt as a sculptor.
I'd use volcanic heat,
water from Fire River,
hot sand from its bed
and I'd sing to my materials.
They'd sing back, glowing.
Even Jivaro headhunters
would be shocked at how easily
I'd slit the sides of each limb,
peel the skin from your neck
and torso down to your feet.
How I'd discard your meat
and ask all my animals
if they were hungry.
The anaconda-canoe would carry
your organs to the feast
while I sewed your seams.
Then I'd boil your skin
and iron it with river-flames.
I'd fill your body-sack with hot sand,
the badness would bubble out.
I wouldn't stop until
you'd shrunk enough to be my doll.
I'd hang you from a hook
and stare at my naked Papa—
your miniature penis
that couldn't hurt a mouse.
I'd take you to a part of the forest
where only children are allowed.
Walking there, I'd listen
to what your soul had to say.

当我来到空旷地
我会把你摆在那儿。留在那儿
当孩子们聚到你周围
耳语着，摸着你细小的手指。

(周瓒 译)

有火蚁的自画像

去拜访你，父亲，我戴了一副火蚁面具。
当我坐下等着你解释

为什么你抛弃我，在我八岁时
火蚁们列队挺进，红色的身体

聚在我双眼周围，螫着我的瞳孔直到它们发白
直到我失明。然后它们袭击我的嘴巴。

我试图舔掉它们，可它们爬下我的喉管
直到完整的一大群叮上我的胃，

而你准是变成了一只食蚁兽，
粘糊糊的长舌头探进我的嗓子，

就像你曾对我幼小的弟弟做过的，
当他假装睡着时给过他法国式亲吻。

我不记得你对我做了什么，但火蚁们知道。

(周瓒 译)

When I arrived at the clearing
I'd lay you out. And stay
as the children gathered around
whispering, touching your tiny fingers.

Self-Portrait with Fire Ants

To visit you Father, I wear a mask of fire ants.
When I sit waiting for you to explain

why you abandoned me when I was eight
they file in, their red bodies

massing around my eyes, stinging my pupils white
until I'm blind. Then they attack my mouth.

I try to lick them but they climb down my gullet
until an entire swarm stings my stomach,

while you must become a giant anteater,
push your long sticky tongue down my throat,

as you once did to my baby brother,
French-kissing him while he pretended to sleep.

I can't remember what you did to me, but the ants know.

蛇屋

到了攀上你前门的时候了，母亲，
按响一只尖利蜂鸣的门铃，
这门有两颗弯曲的尖牙。
我进去，走入门厅那肌肉发达的喉咙，
走下此刻关闭着的地道
见到一点针尖般的灯光。
我置身于正在吞咽般的卧室，
为它洗洗擦擦，半个我活着
仿佛一个准备着祈雨舞的男人
在干燥的河床。他走进
来到矿井中，洗擦抚慰着群蛇
为了稍后当他起舞时将这些"小母亲们"
放在他嘴里，而它们不会咬他。
我是个小孩，呆在游戏围栏内
和我的宠物响尾蛇一起，
喂它们面包和牛奶。
只要我不害怕
它们就不袭击我。而此刻你说道，
"只有小女孩能够做到"。
至今我的脸颊还几乎没有缝合，
无数的移植物隐藏在坏死的部分里。

（周瓒 译）

约束衣

我把手提箱放在父亲的床上
慢慢地，轻柔地打开它。
里面，躺着四十只活蜂鸟
裹着约束衣
拴成几排，每颗小小的脑袋
垫在褴褛般的身子上。
我用一只细颈瓶喂它们糖水，
往每只鸟喙里塞进吸管，
然后解开它们的捆束
好让父亲能够看到它们变幻颜色
它们在他的房间里飞来冲去。
它们在贴近他面孔的上方盘旋

The Snake House

It's time to go up to your front door, Mother,
and ring the rattling buzzer of a bell,
the door with two curved fangs.
I go in, into the muscular throat of the hall,
down the tunnel that's closing now
to a pinpoint of light.
I'm in the swallowing living-room,
washing it for you, half-alive,
like a man preparing for the rain-dance
in the dry arroyo. He reaches
into the pit and washes the snakes
so that later when he dances with the 'little mothers'
in his mouth, they won't bite.
I'm a child playing in the pen
with my pet rattlers,
giving them bread and milk.
As long as I'm unscared
they won't strike. And you're saying,
"Only a girl-child can do this".
My cheeks are almost seamless now,
countless grafts hide the necrosis.

The Strait-Jackets

I lay the suitcase on Father's bed
and unzip it slowly, gently.
Inside, packed in cloth strait-jackets
lie forty live hummingbirds
tied down in rows, each tiny head
cushioned on a swaddled body.
I feed them from a flask of sugar water,
inserting every bill into the pipette,
then unwind their bindings
so Father can see their changing colours
as they dart around his room.
They hover inches from his face

仿佛他是一朵花儿,它们嗡嗡着
刚好在氧气机上方听得到。
我第一次来这里时
他呼吸顺畅,
插管连到他的鼻孔,差不多滑了出来。
我不知道我们坐了多久
但当我再一次扫视他的脸
他睡着了,蜂鸟羽毛上的光芒
依然在他的眼皮和面颊上游动。
我花了几小时将它们全部捉住
并把它们裹进约束衣里。
我安静地做着一切,他睡得
如此之深,一次都没醒来。

*题注:约束衣,指给囚犯或有暴力倾向的精神病患者设计的一种紧身衣。

(周瓒 译)

地图蛾

这只硕大的彩翅蛾
阔翼宛若中国地图。

这里两道长城蜿蜒。那儿
前翼挺出尖尖的满洲

有龙首震慑劫掠者。
但地图上这些鳞片晶亮

邀请着光的窗口是什么?
仿佛大地的皮肤

于薄暮某一瞬敞开。
这嫩嫩斑斓的地图

栖在我手上,它抖动——
热着身,像个新世界,临风欲飞。

(杨炼、张炜 译)

as if he's a flower, their humming
just audible above the oxygen recycler.
For the first time since I've arrived
he's breathing easily, the cannula
attached to his nostrils almost slips out.
I don't know how long we sit there
but when I next glance at his face
he's asleep, lights from their feathers
still playing on his eyelids and cheeks.
It takes me hours to catch them all
and wrap them in their strait-jackets.
I work quietly, he's in such
a deep sleep he doesn't wake once.

Atlas Moth

This giant atlas moth's broad wings
could be the map of China.

Here are two Great Walls. And there
on the Manchurian tip of each forewing

are dragon heads to scare off predators.
But what are those windows in the map,

where crystal scales let in the light?
As if earth's skin has windows

and at certain times of the evening
they open. The newly emerged atlas

perches on my hand, and it trembles—
like a new world, warming up for its first flight.

神奇的语言

我曾精通星际的音乐
而它消隐。我救出一枚音符

保藏在舌下
启动我第一次呼吸。

出生后,我将那音符捣碎成颜色
细细打量这世界——

我们的家,此地我被反锁
在自身的地窖里。

门上一条悬吊的链子,
缀满了颤颤的小铃,

星夜霜霰般叮当作响。
之后,门轻启,我一步踏出

裸身而立
雪花点点在皮肤上融化,

一如失传语言中的词。

(杨炼、张炜 译)

Unearthly Languages

I was fluent in the music of the spheres
but it faded. So I salvaged one note

and kept it under my tongue
to fuel my first breath.

After my birth, I broke that note into colours
with which to see the world—

our home, where I was locked
in the cellar of myself.

The door has a leash hanging from it,
with little bells that shiver,

the way frost tinkles on a starry night.
Then the door clicks open and I go out

and stand naked
while snowflakes melt on my skin,

like the words of a lost language.

镜兰

一座巨蜥山丘高耸在我们的葡萄园之上,
它遍布蛇鳞的蓟叶于午寐中缓缓开合恍若张口欲言。

自幼我仰望,想几个星期不被搅扰地在嶙峋的山脊上行走,
我的嘴大张,我的眼帘半闭,追逐
　　睫毛扑闪的朦胧间水晶兽一闪而过的尾巴。

低处的台地上,葡萄间,石英翼和流星眼的蜻蜓
吹拂高原的香——一朵云,我若不怕就能隐身其中。

此时此地,我攀援巨石的阶梯——
那梯级宽阔如地平线,坠石把我的指节擦破。
每道裂缝是一条铬绿色河谷,我沐浴且脱下予然者十二层惊悸之皮。

直至我终于带着放大镜到了,分开茅草,
金剑叶的蓟头宛如沙漠美杜莎,这化石花有石花瓣与硫磺茎。

甲虫们爬出花冠,顶着虹彩黑的角向我挥舞触须,
　　载满地下航行的传说。
它们看过怎样的紫光宝石?探测过怎样的寂静,
　　从咆哮的阳光漩涡中浮起?
它们被花粉染得金黄,匆匆钻出时,冷风劲吹他们的甲。

有的背着箭簇,瞄准——这边!紧急!紧急!
于是我追随三叶虫的部落,我信他们。
我走至双脚麻木,磨蹭前行像千足虫穿过数千年。

它们把我领向那召唤着一根茎的蓝光——一只小小的、带斑点的翼。
诡秘的女王,黄蜂兰有镜子的性。

The Mirror Orchid

A megasaurian massif reared above our vineyard,
its reptile-scale thistles slowly opening and closing during siestas as if they
    wanted to speak.

Since childhood I looked up, wanting to walk for weeks undisturbed on
    the spiny crest of the great garrigue,
my catching-flies-mouth open, my eyes half-closed, chasing
    the glimpsed tail of a crystalline beast in the blur of my flickering
    eyelashes.

Even down in the terraces, among the vines, dragonflies with quartz wings
    and meteor eyes
brought the perfume of the plateau—a cloud I could vanish in if I dared.

And now here I am climbing the giant stone ladder—
its rungs wide as the horizon, my knuckles grazed by falling rocks.
Each gap a viridian-rivered gorge where I bathe and shed the twelve
    scare-skins of singlehood.

Until at last I arrive with my magnifying glass, parting the straw-grasses,
the golden sword-leafed thistle-heads like desert medusas, the fossil-flowers
    with stone petals and sulphur stems.

Iridescent-black horned beetles crawl out of their corollas and wave
    antennae at me, bearing news from subterranean voyages.
What ultraviolet jewels have they seen? What silences have they plumbed,
    to surface in roaring whirlpools of sunlight?
And the mistral blasting their armour-plates, as they scuttle out, gilded
    with pollen,

some with arrows on their backs, pointing—This way! Urgent! Urgent!
So I follow the trilobite tribe. I trust them.
I walk until my feet are numb, so numb they glide like millipedes across
    millennia.

They lead me to a blue light beckoning on a stem—a tiny, speckled speculum.
The queen of subterfuge, a wasp-orchid with a looking-glass sex.

天空的全部颜料被这苍穹吞食者所包裹，在这液晶屏上
时间一幕幕展开，当我渐渐移近，我的脸被花萼的碗扣紧，

这里连钟乳的分秒也停止了滴落。
这里史前的蝈蝈吟唱石头的歌——我得侧耳才能听到那滴答声。

在它魅惑信息的颠倒的天空中，一支香歌向独一无二的恋人逸出。
我进入中央水晶巢，星工厂，世界窗，天底
那儿茎之隧道拖我向下穿越苍白的根系。

我饮幽独的树液，滚烫如岩浆，凝重如我行星的铁核。

蜂兰在抖动，幼虫数度白热地变形，
化为一只雌黄蜂。她的蓝翼发光
像刚出生的婴儿的胎衣。像簇新的望远镜上完美的镜片。

此刻，光淹没我之前，我必须注视进拉扎克高原多刺的腹地，
那里摇动着虚空的火瓣花。
　　我问候露齿的睡眠之花和它们的授粉者。
　　我问候它们静谧、修长、扎人、螺旋的茎，它们吮大地的根。

穿越夜之内核的黑色面纱，天虫降临。
午夜金龟子，吐血虫，雄壮的摩羯虫和鹿角虫——
所有埋藏我孤独生命的甲虫们。

圆蜘蛛的网是一个岛的星系——
它之字形的网上挂着我未做完的懵懂的梦。

金星镜兰闪亮，她的雄蕊伺伏在我之上
像锤又像刷，我若不逃就再次将我涂抹。

一只黄蜂，或一个情人？被魔法招出花瓣掩映的钴色的长廊，
我听见他趋近，他的翅膀因怯懦的光嗡嗡作响。

All the sky's pigment is packed in this sky-swallower, this plasma screen
where time unreels, frame by frame, as I inch nearer, my face gripped by
    the cave of its calyx,

where even stalactite-seconds have stopped dripping.
Where a prehistoric cicada sings a stone song—a clock-tick my ears must
    tune themselves to.

In the upside-down sky of its pheromone-trap, a scent-song is released
    for only one lover.
I enter the central crystal nest, star-factory, world-window, nadir
where stem-tunnels draw me down through etiolated systems of roots.

I drink the sap of solitude, scalding as magma, heavy as the iron core of
    my planet.

Ophrys miroir is vibrating now, metamorphosing into a female wasp,
passing through incandescent larva stages. Her blue wings shimmer
like the vernix on a newborn baby. Like the flawless lens on a newly cast
    telescope.

And now, before I drown in light, I must peer into the stinging heart of
    the Larzac
where the fire-petalled flowers of the void sway.
    I greet the toothed flowers of sleep and their pollinators.
    I greet their silent, long, thorned, spiral stems, their planet-sucking roots.

Through black veils of night's nucleus, the sky-insects come.
The midnight scarab, the blood-spitter, the great Capricorn and flying stag—
all the burying beetles of my lonely life.

And the orb-spider whose web is an island galaxy—
my swaddled, half-digested dreams dangle from the zigzag that streaks her net.

Mirror of Venus glistens, her stamens poised above me
like hammers or brushes that will repaint me if I don't run.

A wasp, or a lover? Conjured from the long cobalt corridors under the petal,
I hear him approach, his wings humming with nervous light.

阳光的网为他飞向那镜兰助力,花瓣
为我打开如奢华的天蓝色卧榻上一张张床单,
闪耀的阳光下细丝茸茸柔软,我用手触摸,却是一片清凉。

一次又一次,我跌进花粉团的金色雷霆,花粉沾满了我的头。

而我的情人拥抱我,移近如一头雄蜂移向一朵花——
　　陌生的造物朝向陌生的造物。

(杨炼、有玲 译)

Networks of sunrays harnessed for his flight to the mirror-flower, whose petals
are opening for me like the sheets of a plush azure bed,
the velvet nap lithe with solar flares but cool to my touch.

Again and again, the pollinia are stuck to my head as I tumble into their
    gold thunders.

And my lover clasps me, drawing close as a male wasp can draw to a flower—
    alien species to alien species.

菲奥娜·辛普森

共同的祈祷

因为他即便强过整个世界,也无从强过他自身。
　　　　——克尔凯廓尔

柳枝的幡带
飒瑟着——
　　　沉重,飘忽不定——
在今日向西的长风中;
这大洋的咆哮
自远匿的初始以来
　　　　总在肆虐,

你听得见它裹胁的话语
却无从领会,
　　　抗辩
和赋予;
当它穿过本地
刻下它的启示。

吹过衰草萋萋的围场的风
一道
环球的踪迹,
被驱动的行星的
边缘:
被争夺,被锻打的边缘。

　　　　圣坛的铁幕
和灵交的栅栏,隐入一座黑暗的教堂;
跪垫锉磨赤裸的膝盖。
挣扎。祈祷如同绵延的失败。
自我
攀爬疑问
直至坍塌——

　　　上帝
存在于它自身无法逾越的
距离。

Fiona Sampson

Common Prayer

'Because even though he be stronger than the entire world,
he nevertheless is not stronger than himself.'
                    (Kierkegaard)

Streamers of willow
sough—
            grave, elastic—
in today's long-drawn-out Westerly;
this oceanic roar
blowing since the start of something
                                far off,

carrying language you hear
but can't grasp,
            struggle
and give;
the revelation of scale
as it moves through the local.

Wind in the dead grasses of the paddock
a trace
        of the global, rim
of the driven planet:
contested, wrought.

                Screen-iron of sanctuary
and communion rail, in a dark church;
a hassock rasping bare knees.
Struggle. Prayer as continuing failure.
The self
        mounting by questions
to collapse—

            God
was in His own unbridgeable
distance.

你的手指触诊你的眼睑，
星星点缀猩红，
　　　　一片融金的苍穹。

一只松木的棺材摇篮
摇晃且嘟囔着——
没有木头永远沉寂——
当你漂浮在
声音的水面。

　　　　那声音
探测着虚空的上腭
　　　　它曾是你的声音；

在教众中孤孤单单
彼此的回应，
　　　　自你被切断，
互相切断

如同增厚了
彩色窗玻璃的黑暗。

这和从属无关。你一无所属。
这是某种景观
如同忏悔者的景观。

　　　　白色的柳枝
在这玻璃窗格的光盒中来回晃动，

灵魂
擦拭着四月那
黄蓝相间的透镜，
　　　　它那永不能被推断的
散花般的坠落。

不可能效仿
那无法预计的生长的奉献。

但可以把教堂想象成，比如说——
这把伞。

Your fingers palpated your eyelids,
starring the red,
 a firmament of gold.

A pine coffin-cradle
rocked and murmured—
no wood is ever dead—
as you floated
in waters of sound.

 That voice
testing the palate of the void
 was yours;

alone among the congregation
echoing each other,
 cut off from you,
from each other

as dark thickened the glass
of coloured windows.

It's not about belonging. You don't *belong.*
It's about the landscape
as confessor.

 In the light-box of this pane
the white-branched willow moves to and fro,

spirit
 brushing the lens
of yellow-and-blue April,
 its petalled fall
of what can never be concluded.

Impossible to emulate
the unaccountable give of growth.

But think of the Church as, say—
this umbrella.

壁画延展开局部
如同伞肋上丝质的皮肤
　　　　　　　升举，颤栗
沉落

在深深的睡眠中：
当伞柄疾速弹出把手
在雨中点燃它蝴蝶的翅膀，
　　　彩色尼龙优美的八条边
所有的拉力和平衡力
突然开始启动。

漂浮
猛然把你的手臂拉向更高
一种有关升天的暗示。

你就是手臂。犹如你就是伞肋，
精美的石墨被你自身的重量
压成一道下坠的曲线。

雨划破易逝的空气留下丝丝痕迹。
一道彩虹开启。如此之高
它近处的虹脚
近乎垂直
　　设若这样的光明
在大地上行走——

携带着危险和伤害
那大风所暗示的
正是这纪念碑式的立柱；
不是一个父亲
永无信誉的归来

而是后花园里
寻寻觅觅的新郎
　　跟随着私下里
抛下的允诺。

凶猛，慷慨——
或许只是一阵翅膀的抖动——
留住你

Canvas stretches over its parts
like the silk of skin on ribs
                              that lift, shudder
and fall

in deep sleep:
                  the cute octagon of coloured nylon
suddenly at work,
all strain and counterbalance,
when the haft shoots up the handle
firing its butterfly wing at rain.

Afloat,
it tugs your arm higher,
                              a suggestion of levitation.

You are the arm. As you're the ribs,
fine graphite forced in a descending curve
by your own weight.

Rain streaks fugitive air.
A rainbow opens, so high
its near foot
seems vertical.
                  If such brightness
walked the earth—

it's this monumental upright
                              the gale implies
with danger and buffeting;
not a father's
never-believed-in return

but the sought-for bridegroom
privately alight
            with recognition
in the garden.

Feral, generous—
maybe a shudder of wings—
keeping you company

犹自清醒时的交际,
无时不刻,
凝视着木墙上
柳枝的疏影:
　　　　一出戏剧
你永不能领略——

那四月的阳光下
纵横交错的纷纭。

(唐晓渡 译)

while you remain awake,
moment by moment,
watching shadows of willow-twig
on a wooden wall:
                play
you never catch hold of—

the sift of branches
in April sun.

施加彰

底 片

街道上，一个男人拉着一车煤，这景象被永远固定在静止中。
寺庙内，缓慢收缩的快门

放黑暗而不是光亮进来。
我看到一只老鼠逃窜，转过墙脚，一个男人挥着椅子追打。

我看到人们半夜在武汉的街道旁，睡在竹榻上。
一头胀满了气的死猪在水上漂浮。

我看到一个做儿子的微笑在照片里，两年前他坠崖而死；
单元房的每一个房间里都挂着他的照片。

我遇到一个女人，孩提时代出过天花，被她的母亲抛弃；
但她活下来，现有两女一男和一个女婿；

他们住在三个房间里，看同一台彩色电视机。
我看到一个身穿蓝色工作服的男人，他父亲曾是农民，

早年入党，但到文革之时，
他因身居高位而成为红卫兵攻击的对象。

我看到一个女人，她曾试图用针灸针自杀，
但碰巧扎到一个要害穴位，居然治好了她多年的哮喘。

一个中国诗人坚持认为，东西方的根本差别在于
在东方，个人并不相信自己

能够控制命运，而是屈服于命运；
恰如一张底片颠倒了光与暗，

这些话是对在变为隐喻的个人悲剧的单调畅述。
是敏感于光线的胶片银盐冲洗液，

是从地下避弹掩体改造成的电影院里传出的笑声，
是在颐和园公园里的情侣们。

（西川 译）

Arthur Sze

The Negative

A man hauling coal in the street is stilled forever.
Inside a temple, instead of light

a slow shutter lets the darkness in.
I see a rat turn a corner running from a man with a chair trying to smash it,

see people sleeping at midnight in a Wuhan street on bamboo beds,
a dead pig floating, bloated, on water.

I see a photograph of a son smiling who two years ago fell off a cliff
and his photograph is in each room of the apartment.

I meet a woman who had smallpox as a child, was abandoned by her mother
but who lived, now has two daughters, a son, a son-in-law;

they live in three rooms and watch a color television.
I see a man in blue work clothes whose father was a peasant

who joined the Communist party early but by the time of the Cultural
        Revolution
had risen in rank and become a target of the Red Guards.

I see a woman who tried to kill herself with an acupuncture needle
but instead hit a vital point and cured her chronic asthma.

A Chinese poet argues that the fundamental difference between East and West
is that in the East an individual does not believe himself

in control of his fate but yields to it.
As a negative reverses light and dark

these words are prose accounts of personal tragedy becoming metaphor,
an emulsion of silver salts sensitive to light,

laughter in the underground bomb shelter converted into a movie theater,
lovers in the Summer Palace park.

马　脸

狱中，一个男子被人叫"马脸"，但无动于衷，
与此同时裁缝铺中每一个人都手持锋利的冰凉的剪刀；

这男子记住了侮辱但一笑了之。与此同时
一位正在焊钢筋的卡塔罗格斯印第安人

扭头去看与笑声同时发出的叫喊，失脚，
摔死。我打开一瓶啤酒，一辆汽车开近车库。

门打开，一盏灯亮起来，车库内的金属耙子闪闪发光；
一个腹泻的男孩儿在牛尿中洗手。

我找到锯末的踪迹，走进去发现一个死去杀手的
已发硬的破旧皮鞋，体会到感受一瞬间的整个危险

是多么艰难：一匹马产下
小马驹，城市停电，一位舞蹈者

停在黑暗中，努力听寻表演伴奏
却只听到突然的恐慌的叫喊。

(西川 译)

猪西天客栈

红辣椒在捧起阳光的篮子里——
我们趟过一堆烧焦的桑叶走进
西递村，一个院子，注意到
一方石砚，雕着书法，盛满水
和桂花瓣，有味道的明代
红木镶壁板。一位乐师把埙擎到
唇边吹起时，我看见猕猴桃
悬垂于月亮门上方的枝头：
一位曾为妙龄小妾的老祖母，
缩在椅子里，膝盖绑着
绷带，喃喃抱怨病痛；
街上有人啐痰，第二位乐师
拨动古琴的弦，枝头的柚子

Horse Face

A man in prison is called horse face, but does nothing
when everyone in the tailor shop has sharp cold scissors;

he remembers the insult but laughs it off. Even as he
laughs, a Cattaraugus Indian welding a steel girder

turns at a yell which coincides with the laugh and slips
to his death. I open a beer, a car approaches a garage.

The door opens, a light comes on, inside rakes gleam;
a child with dysentery washes his hands in cow piss.

I find a trail of sawdust, walk in a dead killer's
hardened old shoes, and feel how difficult it is to

sense the entire danger of a moment: a horse gives birth
to a foal, power goes out in the city, a dancer

stops in the dark and listening for the noise that was scored
in the performance hears only sudden panicked yells.

Pig's Heaven Inn

Red chillies in a tilted basket catch sunlight—
we walk past a pile of burning mulberry leaves
into Xidi village, enter a courtyard, notice
an inkstone, engraved with calligraphy, filled
with water and cassia petals, smell Ming
dynasty redwood panels. As a musician lifts
a small *xun* to his mouth and blows, I see kiwis
hanging from branches above a moon doorway:
a grandmother, once the youngest concubine,
propped in a chair with bandages around
her knees, complains of incessant pain;
someone spits in the street. As a second
musician plucks strings on a zither, pomelos

更黑了；一位妇人剥开栗子皮；
两个男人在一只平底船上捞
河里的鸭草。音符银亮亮
朝铺路的鹅卵石泼水，我的
手指猝然疼痛。文革间
我姨夫跃出三楼上的
窗户；在清晨，我误把雨声
听成鸟鸣；当乐师暂停，
黄山松附在光明顶近旁
摇曳；一口猪在围栏后蹒跚；
有人擤鼻子。往昔之痕
是一小把桑叶，屋瓦上轻烟袅袅
飘起；在我们也消散前，我们
向三条小径汇合处跋涉：数百人
驻足我们之前，数百人尾随在后：
我们形成人的溪流，送葬
向下穿过花岗岩的洞穴

（杨炼　译）

从圣达菲市加利斯泰欧街回望马柯舒特印第安保留地

马柯舒特独木舟出发驶进海湾，
前头插着神灵保佑的鹰羽和黄色的
雪松枝。一个女孩看着
她母亲在平底锅里煎厚厚的鹿肉片——
血滴嗞啦响，接着蒸发。因为
鹿是邻家所喂，她们默默无言地吃着；
沉默有时打破，当她发出呕声，
把手指伸进喉咙抽出鹿毛。
父亲走了，怒气冲冲地走了，在与他
下班以后开车去靶场的老板争吵过之后；
部落的会计走了，他贪污了基金，
弄来辆小卡车，声称自己是在
老虎机上赢了个同花顺。你捐出
鸡汤和衣物但从未听说它们
是否抵达了城市的南端。你的
微末之举不过是湿沙上矶鹬鸟的爪痕。
报纸、塑料容器、啤酒瓶
塞满这单行下坡道旁的垃圾箱。

（西川　译）

blacken on branches; a woman peels chestnuts;
two men in a flat-bottomed boat gather
duckweed out of a river. The notes splash,
silvery, onto cobblestone, and my fingers
suddenly ache: during the Cultural Revolution,
my aunt's husband leapt out of a third-story
window; at dawn I mistook the cries of
birds for rain. When the musicians pause,
Yellow Mountain pines sway near Bright
Summit Peak; a pig scuffles behind an enclosure;
someone blows his nose. Traces of the past
are wisps of mulberry smoke rising above
roof tiles; and before we too vanish, we hike
to where three trails converge: hundreds
of people are stopped ahead of us, hundreds
come up behind: we form a rivulet of people
funneling down through a chasm in the granite.

Looking Back on the Muckleshoot Reservation from Galisteo Street, Santa Fe

The bow of a Muckleshoot canoe, blessed
with eagle feather and sprig of yellow cedar,
is launched into a bay. A girl watches
her mother fry venison slabs in a skillet—
drops of blood sizzle, evaporate. Because
a neighbor feeds them, they eat wordlessly;
the silence breaks when she occasionally
gags, reaches into her throat, pulls out hair.
Gone is the father, riled, arguing with his boss,
who drove to the shooting range after work;
gone the accountant who embezzled funds,
displayed a pickup, and proclaimed a winning
flush at the casino. You donate chicken soup
and clothes but never learn if they arrive
at the south end of the city. Your small
acts are sandpiper tracks in wet sand.
Newspapers, plastic containers, beer bottles
fill the bins along this sloping one-way street.

混沌初开

画家在静物中展现时间
下午的斜阳照亮了一把刀
几个柠檬、绿瓶里剩余的红酒
我们总留一些干不完的东西?
想要的得到了,
又想拿什么X、Y、Z?
我试着在一个柠檬切片的反光中
感受混沌初开的时分
我向泥水扔着小石头
希望这样能与饥饿连接
"吃吧"一位来自阿富汗的人说
指着打开的车后厢里又老又烂的苹果
我看到一队男人跳着云层的舞
两头各有一个女人扭着复杂的闪电舞步
我的许多失败与错误甚至像欢乐的时刻
在我的心中颤动不已
但我希望光明的时刻
能像印尼的编锣那样共鸣
我愿能把我们生活中紧密而奇异的时刻
镶成玉石、黑曜石、绿松石、
黑檀木和天青石的地板

(严力 译)

The Moment of Creation

A painter indicates the time of day
in a still life: afternoon light slants on a knife,
lemons, green wine bottle with some red wine.
We always leave something unfinished?
We want x and having x want y and having y want z?
I try to sense the moment of creation
in the shine on a sliced lemon. I want to
connect throwing gravel on mud to being hungry.
"Eat," a man from Afghanistan said
and pointed to old rotting apples in the opened car trunk.
I see a line of men dancing a cloud dance;
two women dance intricate lightning steps
at either end. My mistakes and failures
pulse in me even as moments of joy,
but I want the bright moments to resonate out
like a gamelan gong. I want to make
the intricate tesselated moments of our lives
a floor of jade, obsidian, turquoise, ebony, lapis.

乔治·塞尔特斯

水
乔治　塞尔特斯 原作

水之法则美丽而坚硬：
用排水量升起，反衬人
和他的家之无能。它否认
预谋或欺骗。遇冷封冻；
热了蒸发。它携带病菌
与河海中亮丽聪颖的鱼群。
嘶叫或闲逛在都市街区
天、树和楼群倒映其中。

它涤净并刷新我们甚而当我们
囚于浴盆或在掩体中颤栗或不顾
一切狂奔进情人的臂弯，那一刻
耗子们也在逃窜。它静静延伸
领地。背弓起太阳下一个圆弧
唯一遵循着坚硬的水的法则。

(杨炼 译)

George Szirtes

Water

The hard beautiful rules of water are these:
That it shall rise with displacement as a man
does not, nor his family. That it shall have no plan
or subterfuge. That in the cold, it shall freeze;
in the heat, turn to steam. That it shall carry disease
and bright brilliant fish in river and ocean.
That it shall roar or meander through metropolitan
districts whilst reflecting skies, buildings and trees.

And it shall clean and refresh us even as we slave
over stone tubs or cower in a shelter or run
into the arms of a loved one in some desperate quarter
where the rats too are running. That it shall have
dominion. That it shall arch its back in the sun
only according to the hard rules of water.

疯人院

疯人院的要点在它雄性十足。
疯人院的要点在它被信仰卡住了。
疯人院的要点在心智是老板。
疯人院的要点在没人行动。
疯人院的要点在没人能仅凭友善入门。
疯人院的要点在它解放精神。
疯人院的要点在那里你能专心想你喜欢的事儿。
疯人院的要点在谁都能进去。
疯人院没什么特别人们任何时候随意进出。
疯人院没什么威胁,我们都在死去。
疯人院没什么悲哀,哭泣和咬牙不算什么。
疯人院没什么疯狂,它的心智是拖延。
我们的健全靠拖延维系,疯狂靠设计,疯才被赏识。
被赏识是猿猴,是波斯枭鸟,细胞,咽喉红肿,
被赏识是兰花,是大蒜,是合紧书本里的火,
赏识拷打的嚎哭,夜莺丢失的声音,爆笑
穿着每件小东西装正常但理智正奔向疯狂
就像阳光,慢腾腾的火车,耷拉的每一滴,大马路,
满溢的眼睛,影子,野餐,公共运输,雷霆。
自然用秩序及它的爱好者们疯了。
文化疯了每个人都在遗传它。
科学用对数字的爱疯了,一种完美的纵情私通。
健康疯了从一分钟疯向下一分钟,肌肉大大的!
钱疯了塞满你的口袋在花园里甩下银质拉拉蛄尾巴。
疯人院的要点是别谈论它。
疯人院的要点是别改变它。
疯人院的要点是住在那儿,
习惯你自己修饰完美的举止,
永远住进主子的房子
伴陪先知,诗人,侏儒,学者,火。

(杨炼 译)

Madhouse

The point about the madhouse is that it's virile.
The point about the madhouse is that it sticks by its beliefs.
The point about the madhouse is that sanity is bourgeois.
The point about the madhouse is that no one is acting.
The point about the madhouse is that no one gets in by simply being nice.
The point about the madhouse is that it liberates the spirit.
The point about the madhouse is that you can think just what you like there.
The point about the madhouse is that anyone can enter.
There's nothing special about the madhouse, people come and go all the time.
There's nothing threatening about the madhouse, we are all of us dying.
There's nothing terminal about the madhouse: you go along for the ride.
There's nothing sad about the madhouse: weeping and gnashing of teeth,
    that's nothing.
There's nothing mad about the madhouse, it is sanity by default.
We are sane by default, we are mad by design, but the mad are more
    admirable.
Admirable is the ape, the bulbul, the mitochondria, the swelling of the
    larynx,
Admirable the orchid, the garlic, the fire inside the shut book,
Admirable the cry of the tortured, the lost voice of the nightingale, the
    laughter
in everything ostensibly sane but tending towards madness
such as sunlight, the slow rain, each pendulous drop, the wide road,
the brimming eye, shadows, picnics, public conveyances, thunder.
Nature is a madness with a method and all the madder for that.
Culture is a madness everyone inherits.
Science is a madness in love with numbers, the perfect *amour fou*.
Health is a madness that shifts from minute to minute, *gesundheit!*
Money is madness that fills your pockets and leaves a silver slugtrail in
    the garden.
The point about the madhouse is not to describe it.
The point about the madhouse is not to change it.
The point about the madhouse is to live there,
to accustom yourself to its immaculate manners,
to dwell in the house of the Lord for ever
with the prophet, the poet, the dwarf, the scholar, the fire.

只要可以我们时刻地纵情生活
(仿马茂德·达维什,给咪咪·卡尔瓦第)

只要可以我们时刻地纵情生活。
我们天天进杂货店、面包店
　药店和邮局。
只要可以我们时刻地纵情生活。
我们借彼此的书和纸夹
并不记得退。
我们精心打扮,叫的士,钻进巴士或火车
去开一个会。
只要可以我们时刻地纵情生活
因此我们签署信件和卡片
夜里上街遛弯
当冬天冷极而窗户里面
和游乐场里面灯光对着黑暗
低吼而且大海静静地
咀嚼悬崖而且猫头鹰、耗子和狐狸动来
动去我们听见并且听着。
只要可以我们时刻地纵情生活。

(萧开愚 译)

所有可能的世界里最好的那个

所有可能的世界里最好的那个在过夜
已在床上睡着。
梦见一英里深的雪。

所有可能的世界里最好的那个在窥视
镜子里的自己,
眼睛如两个大盘子。

所有可能的世界里最好的那个在巴士站里
在连绵的雨里,
观看降水,一滴一滴。

所有可能的世界里最好的那个已厌弃
枯等那承诺过的改善。
已经没有想要的东西。

We love life whenever we can
(For Mimi Khalvati, after Mahmoud Darwish)

We love life whenever we can.
We enter the grocer's, the baker's, the chemist's
   the post office daily.
We love life whenever we can.
We borrow each other's books and paperclips
   and forget to return them.
We spruce ourselves up for a meeting, order
   a taxi, climb into a bus or a train.
We love life whenever we can
   and so we sign letters and cards and spend
   the evening walking the street
When the winter is fiercest and the light
   in the windows and amusement arcades
   snarls at the darkness and the sea is quietly chomping at
   the cliff and the owl and the rat and the fox move over and
   through and we hear them and listen.
We love life whenever we can.

The Best of All Possible Worlds

The best of all possible worlds is asleep
having turned in for the night.
It is dreaming of snow a mile deep.

The best of all possible worlds contemplates
its own reflection in the mirror,
its eyes two enormous plates.

The best of all possible worlds is at the bus stop
in a steady shower of rain
watching water fall, drop by drop.

The best of all possible worlds is tired
of waiting for the promised improvements.
It has run out of things to be desired.

所有可能的世界里最好的那个变成
一个紧张，笨蛋的空想，
手笨脚也笨。

所有可能的世界里最好的那个是颗黑星
在自己加工的宇宙里，
嘟囔：万事本来的样子就挺称心。

万事本来的样子就挺称心，墙头的阳光说
万事本来的样子就挺称心，骨中的寒冷说
万事在所有可能的世界里最好的那个中的本来的样子就挺称心哟。

(萧开愚 译)

关于蛇的一些谚语
(仿海伦．罗素)

蛇是虚构的，即使在现实中。
我们从一根丝带的卷曲知悉它。
我们从它的移动、眼睛和尖牙知悉它。
我们从感觉到梦到它的恐惧知悉它。
蛇随着黎明第一道光线抵达。
它进入耳朵而从肚脐出来。
它盘绕在肠子和心脏里。
蛇是草中原始的尖叫。
它盘绕在人和树的枝干。
它住在负疚良心的石头下面。
它是项链臂章镯子和歌曲。
蛇是空心管子中的空气。
蛇丈量时间如人类丈量布匹。
蛇在沙子里拼出它的名字。
蛇住在生活的边缘。
当蛇进入一本书，书即关闭。

(萧开愚 译)

The best of all possible worlds becomes
a nervous, clumsy abstraction
all fingers and thumbs.

The best of all possible worlds is a dark star
in a universe of its own making,
muttering: things are fine as they are.

Things are fine as they are, says the sun on the wall
Things are fine as they are, says the cold in the bones
Things are fine as they are in the best of all possible worlds.

Some Sayings about the Snake
After Helen Rousseau

The snake is imaginary, even in life.
We know it from a ribbon by its windings.
We know it by its movement, eyes, and fangs.
We know it from the apprehension we feel dreaming of it.
The snake arrives at dawn with the first light.
It enters through the ear and exits through the navel.
It coils itself within the gut and heart.
The snake is the primal scream in the grass.
It coils around the limbs of man and tree.
It lives under a stone in the guilty conscience.
It is necklace and armlet and bangle and song.
The snake is the air in a hollow tube.
The snake measures time the way man measures cloth.
The snake spells out its name in the sand.
The snake lives at the edges of life.
When the snake enters a book, the book closes.

约书亚·维尔纳

寻回的信

啥让日子更快活？乔戏，瞧这儿：
免费礼品，不是你赚的；
与妻儿的奔放爱意；
冬天扫烟囱，夏日有张好帘子；
法院里几天，捱等小后果；
静静的心，壮壮的躯体，短短地
上班；说真话的密友；
简洁的美食；记忆丰富得
够奠定未来；一张床能
爱，读，梦，再想象爱；
一片暖而干的田野躺下睡，
而睡眠修剪趋近的长夜；
懂得你是谁，不想是
别个；任意忘掉时间；
感知灵魂逾越了界限，
还不在乎释放它的条款，
像孩子的风筝放进风中
飞，因为手拽着那根线。

(杨炼 译)

Joshua Weiner

Found Letter

What makes for a happier life, Josh, comes to this:
Gifts freely given, that you never earned;
Open affection with your wife and kids;
Clear pipes in winter, in summer screens that fit;
Few days in court, with little consequence;
A quiet mind, a strong body, short hours
In the office; close friends who speak the truth;
Good food, cooked simply; a memory that's rich
Enough to build the future with; a bed
In which to love, read, dream, and re-imagine love;
A warm dry field for laying down in sleep,
And sleep to trim the long night coming;
Knowledge of who you are, the wish to be
None other; freedom to forget the time;
To know the soul exceeds where it's confined,
Yet does not seek the terms of its release,
Like a child's kite catching at the wind
That flies because the hand holds tight the line.

蛐蛐

蛐蛐说
你靠摩擦了解蛐蛐,
　而蛐蛐靠音调了解你,

空虚的情人,玩游戏
用甜蜜的呻吟密封那时刻。
看蛐蛐

跳过你丑陋的瓷砖地
和你的靴子嬉戏
当它又砸偏了。

我是蛐蛐,比咖啡和
烟草汁更黑,我的歌
　更苦,更沙哑

只消你暂停打字
闭嘴一分钟。
蛐蛐说

你的双唇拒绝这主意,
蛐蛐的长天线拾起一切,
蛐蛐知道蛐蛐在哪儿。

　蛐蛐用前臂掘洞
嚼你的纸。蛐蛐说
别紧张那结果,

蛐蛐舒展在草从里。
蛐蛐绝不在烟腾腾的室内
悲悲戚戚。

蛐蛐能呼吸。
蛐蛐在你密封的石屋
外面唱。

(杨炼 译)

Cricket

    Cricket says
you know cricket by my rubbing
    and cricket knows you by a like tune,

    vain lovers, playing games
of sweet moan to seal the hour.
    Watch cricket

    leap across your ugly tile floor
and play to your boot
    as it misses once again.

    I'm cricket, blacker than coffee
and tobacco juice, my song
    more bitter, more buzz

    if you'd only quit your typing
and shut up a minute.
    Cricket says

    your lips confuse the issue,
cricket's long antennae pick it all up,
    cricket knows where cricket is.

    Cricket burrows with forelegs,
chews your paper. Cricket says
    stop straining for effect.

    Cricket loves a napper in the grass.
Cricket is never wretched.
    In a room of smoke

    cricket can breathe.
Cricket sings outside
    your sealed room of stone.

Acknowledgements

The English poems reprinted here originally appeared as follows. All appear by permission of the authors, and/or their publishers, as detailed below. Poems not mentioned below are previously uncollected, or have passed back into their author's control, and copyright belongs to their authors © 2013.

Nick Admussen: Both poems are from *Movie-Plots* (New York, NY: Epiphany Editions 2010). Copyright © Nicholas Admussen, 2010.

Tony Barnstone: 'Worn' from *Sad Jazz* (Riverdale-on-Hudson, NY: Sheep Meadow Press 2005); 'Break Up with Him (A How-to Manual)' is from the chapbook, *Naked Magic* (Charlotte, NC: Main Street Rag 2002); 'Hair' is from *Impure* (Gainesville, FL: University Press of Florida 1999). Copyright © Tony Barnstone, 1999, 2002, 2005.

Polly Clark: 'My Life, the Sea', 'Cheng Du Massage', 'Beijing', 'Swan', 'Women' from *Take Me With You* (Tarset: Bloodaxe Books 2005); 'My Education at the Zoo' and 'My Life With Horses' from *Kiss* (Bloodaxe Books 2000). Copyright © Polly Clark, 2000, 2005.

Antony Dunn: All three poems are from *Bugs* (Manchester: Carcanet/OxfordPoets 2009). Copyright © Antony Dunn, 2009.

W. N. Herbert: 'Ghost' is from *Omnesia* (Tarset: Bloodaxe Books 2013); 'A Midsummer Light's Nighthouse', 'Forgive the Flies', 'Border Cow' 'Santiniketan' and 'Tyne Tunnel' are from *Bad Shaman Blues* (Bloodaxe Books 2006); 'Slow Animals Crossing' is from *Big Bumper Book of Troy* (Bloodaxe Books 2002); 'A Difficult Horse' is from *Cabaret McGonagall* (Newcastle: Bloodaxe Books 1996). Copyright © W.N. Herbert 1996, 2002, 2005, 2013

Sean O'Brien: 'Cities', 'Europeans' and 'Tables and Chairs' are taken from *Collected Poems* (London: Picador 2012); 'Another Country' is previously uncollected but first appeared in the anthology, *Jubilee Lines: 60 Poets for 60 Years* (ed. Carol Ann Duffy, London: Faber & Faber, 2012). Copyright © Sean O'Brien, 2001, 2011, 2012.

Pascale Petit: 'My Father's Body', 'Self-Portrait with Fire Ants' and 'The Strait-Jackets' from *The Zoo Father* (Bridgend: Seren 2001); 'The Mirror Orchid', 'Unearthly Languages' and 'The Snake House' from *The Huntress* (Seren 2005); 'Atlas Moth' from *The Treekeeper's Tale* (Seren, 2008). Copyright © Pascale Petit, 2001, 2005, 2008.

Fiona Sampson: 'Common Prayer' from *Common Prayer*, (Manchester: Carcanet Press 2007). Copyright © Fiona Sampson, 2007.

ARTHUR SZE: 'The Negative', 'Horse Face', and 'The Moment of Creation' from *The Redshifting Web: Poems 1970-1998*. Copyright © 1994 by Arthur Sze. 'Pig's Heaven Inn', and 'Looking Back on the Muckleshoot Reservation from Galisteo Street, Santa Fe' from *The Ginkgo Light*. Copyright © 2009 by Arthur Sze. All used by permission of The Permissions Company, Inc., on behalf of Copper Canyon Press, www.coppercanyonpress.org.

GEORGE SZIRTES: 'We love life whenever we can', 'The Best of All Possible Worlds' and 'Some Sayings about the Snake' from *Bad Machine* (Tarset: Bloodaxe Books 2013); 'Water' from *New and Collected Poems* (Bloodaxe Books 2008); 'Madhouse' from *The Burning of the Books and other poems* (Bloodaxe Books 2004). Copyright © George Szirtes, 2004, 2008, 2013.

JOSHUA WEINER: 'Found Letter' and 'Cricket' are from *From the Book of Giants* (Chicago, IL: University of Chicago Press 2006). Copyright © 2006 by The University of Chicago. All rights reserved.

Index of Translators into English

Nick Admussen [NA] [安敏轩]　　　　117-119
Polly Clark [PC] [波丽．克拉克]　　127
Antony Dunn [AD] [安东尼．邓恩]　　45; 69-71; 83
Murray Edmond [ME] [莫瑞 艾德蒙德]　115
John Gery [JG] [约翰 杰瑞]　　　　101-111
Eleanor Goodman [EG] [顾爱玲]　　　43
W.N. Herbert [WNH]
　　[威廉．赫伯特]　　　　　　　47-49; 71-73; 81; 91-95; 113; 129
Brian Holton [BH] [霍布恩]　　　　11-16; 91
Sean O'Brien [SO] [肖恩．奥布莱恩]　125
Pascale Petit [PP] [帕斯卡尔．帕蒂]　53-61; 67; 75; 85-9; 121-5; 131
Fiona Sampson [FS] [菲奥娜．辛普森]　51
Arthur Sze [AS] [施加彰]　　　　　41; 77-9
George Szirtes [GS] [乔治．塞尔特斯]　63-65
Joshua Weiner [JW] [约书亚．维尔纳]　97-99

Index of Translators into Chinese

明迪 [Ming Di]　　　　　　　136-8
唐晓渡 [Tang Xiaodu]　　　　146; 158; 166-8; 200-6
西川 [Xi Chuan]　　　　　　176-8; 208-210; 212
萧开愚 [Xiao Kaiyu]　　　　 220-2
严力 [Yan Li]　　　　　　　 214
杨炼 [Yang Lian]　　　　　　140; 142; 154; 156; 160; 170-4;
　　　　　　　　　　　　　　　 180-2; 190-8; 210; 216-8; 224-6
臧棣 [Zang Di]　　　　　　　134, 138
翟永明 [Zhai Yongming]　　　144-6
周瓒 [Zhou Zan]　　　　　　 148-152; 156; 162-4; 184-8

Index of Poets

姜涛 (1970–) Jiang Tao	40-41
冷霜 (1973–) Leng Shuang	42-43
唐晓渡 (1954–) Tang Xiaodu	44-51
王小妮 (1955–) Wang Xaoni	52-61
西川 (1963–) Xi Chuan	62-71
萧开愚 (1960–) Xiao Kaiyu	72-77
严力 (1954–) Yan Li	78-81
杨炼 (1955–) Yang Lian	82-99
杨小滨 (1963–) Yang Xiaobin	100-111
于坚 (1954–) Yu Jian	112-113
臧棣 (1964–) Zang Di	114-121
翟永明 (1955–) Zhai Yongming	122-125
张炜 (1955–) Zhang Wei	126-127
周瓒 (1968–) Zhou Zan	128-131

§

Nick Admussen (1978–) 安敏轩	134-135
Tony Barnstone (1961–) 托尼．巴恩斯通	136-139
Breyten Breytenbach (1939–) 汴庭博	140-141
Polly Clark (1968–) 波丽．克拉克	142-153
Jennifer Crawford (1975–) 简妮芬．克劳馥	154-155
Antony Dunn (1973–) 安东尼．邓恩	156-159
W.N. Herbert (1961–) 威廉．赫伯特	160-175
Sean O'Brien (1952–) 肖恩．奥布莱恩	176-183
Pascale Petit (1953–) 帕斯卡尔．帕蒂	194-199
Fiona Sampson (1963–) 菲奥娜．辛普森	200-207
Arthur Sze (1950–) 施加彰	208-215
George Szirtes (1948–) 乔治．塞尔特斯	216-223
Joshua Weiner (1963—) 约书亚．维尔纳	224-227

www.ingramcontent.com/pod-product-compliance
Lightning Source LLC
Chambersburg PA
CBHW032127160426
43197CB00008B/544